The Key to Revelation

Inscribed by

[signature]

For _George T. Dailey_

February, 2008

Number _167_

The Key To Understanding The Revelation

Structural Analysis and Commentary

By Dr. Louis Arnold

Arnold Publications
2440 Bethel Road
Nicholasville, Kentucky 40356

The Key To Understanding The Revelation

@ 2008 Louis Arnold
Published by Arnold Publications
First printing, January, 2008
Library of Congress Card Number: 2007904874

ISBN: 978-0-9727188-6-8

Printed in the United States of America
Arnold Publications
2440 Bethel Road
Nicholasville, Kentucky 40356
Phone 1(859)858-3538
Toll free 1(800)854-8571

Contents

Introduction

*T*he Revelation is an awesome Book. In 22 chapters John wrote about earth, Heaven and hell. He wrote about good and evil, and about the conflict of the ages. He wrote about the church, about Israel, and about the Gentile nations. He wrote about good angels, fallen angels, Satan, and the Antichrist, and he wrote about the final battle between Satan and his armies and almighty God. After that he gives a preview of Heaven and the glory that awaits the children of God. Most of all The Revelation is about Jesus.

So much is covered in The Revelation it is difficult to understand when studied as a whole. It is much easier to understand when it is divided into sections and the sections are studied one at a time.

All of the Bible is either written to or written about one of three classes of people: the Jews, the Gentiles, and the church. That is true in The Revelation. Events relating to these three classes are covered in separate sections. A list of all the sections follows.

Section one covers future events from the viewpoint of the church. It is contained in chapters 1 through 6.

Section two covers future events from the viewpoint of Israel. It is contained in chapters 7 through 11.

Section three does not contain any symbols of judgment, such as seals, trumpets, or vials of wrath. Instead, it contains a series of visions that reach back in time to the fall of Satan and forward in time to the reaping of the harvest of the earth. It is contained in chapters 12 through 15.

Section four covers future events, leading up to and including the Second Coming of Christ from the Gentile viewpoint. It is contained in chapters 16 through 19.

Section five covers some end-time events not covered in the other chapters, and it gives the greatest view of the new Heaven and the new earth that is found in the Bible. This section is contained in the last three chapters of The Revelation.

The Authorship of The Revelation

There are those who question that the Apostle John was the author of The Revelation. They insist that some other John may have been the author, but there is considerable evidence that the Apostle John did write the book.

It is certain that the book was written by someone named John. His name is given in the book three times. He gave his name twice in chapter 1, verses 4 and 9, and once in chapter 22, verse 8. That time he stated that he had seen and heard the things he had written about. There is no other well-known John mentioned in the New Testament who could have been the author.

Authorities believe that The Revelation was written in A.D. 96. Dr. H. A. Ironside, in his book entitled, *Revelation,* states: "The traditional view is that the date of the book is A.D. 96." That date appears to be correct. Irenaeus, the friend of Polycarp, who knew John, stated that, "The Revelation was seen at Patmos at the end of Domitian's reign." Domitian reigned from A.D. 81 to 96. Clement of Alexandria left the testimony that John returned from his exile on the death of Domitian in the year 96.

For the first two centuries of the church age the authorship of the Apostle was not questioned. In the third century, some who wanted to undermine the authority of the book, ascribed it to Cerinthus, a reputed first century heretic.

Many of the church fathers believed that the Apostle John wrote The Revelation. Included among them are Justin Martyr, Irenaeus,

Tertullian, Hippolytus, Clement of Alexandria, Origen, Jerome, and Augustine. Justin Martyr frankly stated, "And with us a man named John, one of the apostles of Christ, who in the revelation made to him . . ." *(Dialogue with Trypho the Jew, chapter 81)*.

Of more recent date, a book found in Egypt called *The Apocryphom of John* (about A.D. 150), attributes The Revelation to John, the brother of James. Those who doubt that the Apostle John was the author have no conclusive evidence that he did not write the book.

A Book of Numbers

The Revelation is a book of numbers. The numbers two, three, four, six, seven, twelve, and twenty-four are all mentioned in the book. The number seven is mentioned more often than any other number.

Several writers have used seven sevens as an outline of the book. Scofield lists six sevens in the Scofield Bible as follows.

1. The seven seals
2. The seven trumpets
3. The seven personages
4. The seven vials
5. The seven dooms
6. The seven new things

He gives credit to William J. Erdman for this

list, then adds that the seven churches would make a list of seven sevens. Clarence Larkin gave the same list in his book, *The Book of Revelation,* only he lists the seven churches at the beginning.

Though this list has been often used by others, it is contrived. The seven dooms in the list are not mentioned in The Revelation. The seven personages and seven new things are mentioned, but the number of neither is given in the text.

The structure of The Revelation is woven around a series of nineteen sevens. A different list of seven sevens can easily be made from these. They are (1) the seven churches, (2) the seven candlesticks, (3) the seven stars, (4) the seven spirits of God, (5) the seven lamps of fire, (6) the seven seals, (7) the seven trumpets, (8) the seven vials, (9) the seven angels, (10) the seven eyes, (11) the seven horns, (12) the seven thunders, (13) the seven thousand slain men, (14) the seven heads, (15) the seven crowns, (16) the seven last plagues, (17) the seven mountains, (18) the seven kings, and (19) the seven beatitudes.

The Seven Beatitudes

The seven beatitudes in The Revelation tell us that God has blessings for His people, even in the midst of tribulation.

Beatitude #1

Blessed is he that readeth, and they that hear

the words of this prophecy, and keep those things which are written therein: for the time is at hand (Rev. 1:3).

Beatitude #2

. . . Blessed are the dead which die in the Lord from henceforth . . . (Rev. 14:13).

Beatitude #3

. . . Blessed is he that watcheth, and keepeth his garments, lest he walk naked, and they see his shame (Rev. 16:15).

Beatitude #4

. . . Blessed are they which are called unto the marriage supper of the Lamb . . . (Rev. 19:9).

Beatitude #5

Blessed and holy is he that hath part in the first resurrection: on such the second death hath no power, but they shall be priests of God and of Christ, and shall reign with him a thousand years (Rev. 20:6).

Beatitude #6

. . . blessed is he that keepeth the sayings of the prophecy of this book (Rev. 22:7).

Beatitude #7

Blessed are they that do his commandments . . . (Rev. 22:14).

Chapter 1

A Summary of Chapters 1 Through 6

*C*hapter 1 gives an introduction to the book. Chapters 2 and 3 take us through the church age. Chapter 4 gives a picture of the rapture of the church and the events that will follow in Heaven. Chapter 5 presents the seven-sealed book that only the Lamb of God can open. Chapter 6 takes us through the tribulation for the first time and brings us to the judgment of the Second Coming of Christ.

These events are described in verses 12 through 17 of chapter 6. Verses 12 through 14 tell of signs in the sun, moon, and stars and of the heavens being rolled together like a scroll. These events were predicted by Jesus. Mark 13:24 and 25 tell us that signs in the sun, moon, and stars will occur after the tribulation. *"But in those days, after that tribulation, the sun shall be darkened, and the moon shall not give her light, And the stars of heaven shall fall . . ."* Verse 26 tells us that the Second Coming will follow these events. *"And then shall they see the Son of man coming in the clouds with great power and glory."*

The Second Coming of Christ will be a day of wrath. Paul tells us that Jesus will come with flaming fire, and take vengeance on the ungodly.

". . . the Lord Jesus shall be revealed from heaven with his mighty angels, In flaming fire taking vengeance on them that know not God . . ." (2 Thess. 1:7, 8).

Verses 15 through 17 of Revelation 6 say that men will hide in the dens of the earth when they see the Lord coming and know that the great day of His wrath has come.

Contents of Chapter 1

1. The Revelation of Jesus Christ (verse 1)
2. The future to be revealed in three ways (verse 2)
3. A blessing promised (verse 3)
4. John's salutation (verse 4)
5. Christ identified (verses 5, 6)
6. Christ's visible Second Coming (verse 7)
7. Jesus is eternal (verse 8)
8. The place of John's vision (verse 9)
9. John in the Spirit (verse 10)
10. John's commission to write (verse 11)
11. John's vision of the glorified Lord (verses 12-15)
12. The meaning of the seven stars (verse 16)
13. The glorious presence of the Lord (verse 17)
14. The keys of death and hell (verse 18)
15. The threefold divisions of the book (verse 19)
16. Mystery of the stars and candlesticks (verse 20)

1 The Revelation of Jesus Christ, which God gave unto him, to shew unto his servants things which must shortly come to pass; and he sent and signified it by his angel unto his servant John:

The book of Revelation is a revelation of Jesus Christ. In chapter 1 He is the Alpha and Omega and the glorified Lord in the midst of His churches. In chapters 2 and 3 He is the author of the seven letters to the seven churches. In chapter 5 He is the slain Lamb who is worthy to open the seven-sealed book. Chapter 6 tells of the great day of His wrath. In chapter 7 the Lamb feeds the martyred saints, leads them to fountains of living water, and wipes all tears from their eyes. In chapter 10 He is the mighty angel that stands upon the land and the sea and proclaims the end of delay. Chapter 11 announces that the kingdoms of the world have become the kingdoms of Christ. In chapter 12 He is the Man Child. In chapter 14 He is the Reaper. In chapter 19 He is the Bridegroom and the rider upon a white horse. In chapter 21 He is the light of the new Jerusalem, and in chapter 22 He is the soon coming King.

The Revelation is not a concealing; it is a revealing. It is not a book for the unsaved or the carnal minded. They cannot understand it, but it can be understood by the servants of God. Its purpose is to show the servants of God the things that will soon come to pass.

The Future to be Revealed in Three Ways

2 Who bare record of the word of God, and of the testimony of Jesus Christ, and of all things that he saw.

Verse 2 is a key verse. It tells us that everything in The Revelation is based upon one of three things, the Word of God, the testimony of Jesus Christ, and the visions that John saw.

A Blessing Promised

3 Blessed is he that readeth, and they that hear the words of this prophecy, and keep those things which are written therein: for the time is at hand.

A blessing is promised to those who read The Revelation and to those who hear it read. Those who teach the book have an opportunity to be a blessing to all who hear them.

John's Salutation

4 JOHN to the seven churches which are in Asia: Grace be unto you, and peace, from him which is, and which was, and which is to come; and from the seven Spirits which are before his throne.

After giving his name, John addresses the book to the seven churches in Asia. Then he hastens to add that the book is from the eternal Christ and from the seven spirits that are before His throne. The seven spirits before the throne are called seven lamps (Rev. 4:5).

The lamps are sent into a dark world to make it possible to see what is happening. In Revelation 5:6 we are told that the eyes of the Lamb are the seven Spirits of God that are sent into all the earth. The eyes are for seeing what is taking place in the earth.

Most commentaries say that the seven spirits represent the sevenfold fullness of the Holy Spirit, but the Bible does not say that. These seven spirits may be seven special angels. The Bible says that angels are spirits (Psa. 104:4 and Heb. 1:7). Some angels are sent into the world as observers. There is an obscure reference to angels in 1 Peter 1:12 that says angels desire to look into what is being preached. Perhaps they report what is being preached back to Heaven. That should cause those who preach to be careful that they preach only the message that God gives them.

Christ Identified

5 And from Jesus Christ, who is the faithful witness, and the first begotten of the dead, and the prince of the kings of the earth. Unto him that loved us, and washed us from our sins in his own blood,

6 And hath made us kings and priests unto God and his father; to him be glory and dominion for ever and ever. Amen.

Christ is identified in verses 5 and 6 in seven ways. (1) He is the faithful witness. (2) He is the first begotten of the dead. (3) He is the prince of the kings of the earth. (4) He loved us when we were yet in our sins. (5) He washed us from our sins in His own blood. (6) He has made us kings and priests. (7) He is worthy of praise and glory.

Verse 6 tells us that we are already kings and priests, but we will not serve as such until Christ returns to the earth in His glory. By faith we can now give Him glory for the everlasting kingdom that is to come.

Christ's Visible Second Coming

7 Behold, he cometh with clouds; and every eye shall see him, and they also which pierced him: and all kindreds of the earth shall wail because of him. Even so, Amen.

Verse 7 predicts that every eye will see Jesus in His Second Coming. Modern technology has made it possible for people all over the world to see the Lord on television when He comes, but there will be primitive tribes that will not have television. There will have to be another way for every eye to see Christ's Second Coming.

A mighty host will accompany Christ in His Second Coming, and there will be no way that anyone on earth can miss seeing that glorious event. In Revelation 19:14 John wrote that he saw Jesus coming with the armies of Heaven. The prophet, Zechariah, predicted that all the saints will accompany Jesus in His Second Coming.

". . . and the LORD my God shall come, and all the saints with thee" (Zech. 14:5).

Matthew 25:31 tells us that all the holy angels will come with Jesus. *"When the Son of man shall come in his glory, and all the holy angels with him, then shall he sit upon the throne of his glory."*

Taken together these passages tell us that all the saints of all ages and all the innumerable angels will accompany Christ in His Second Coming. That mighty company will be visible all around the earth.

In the early eighteen hundreds the naturalist, Audubon, reported that migrating Passenger Pigeons, in flocks a mile wide and 300 miles long, darkened the sky for days at a time. Such a flock of birds cannot compare with the trillions of saints and angels that will accompany our Lord on His Second Coming. It will be impossible for anyone on earth to miss seeing the Second Coming of our Lord. His coming will darken the sun and cause the moon to cease from shining. We have already cited the prophecy of Mark about the darkening of the sun and moon. Matthew tells us that this will happen immediately following the tribulation. *"Immediately after the tribulation of those days shall the sun be darkened, and the moon shall not give her light . . ." (Matt. 24:29).*

Jesus is Eternal

8 I am <u>Alpha and Omega, the beginning and the ending, saith the Lord,</u> which is, and which was, and which is to come, the Almighty.

Alpha and Omega, the first and last letters of the Greek alphabet, are used to show that Jesus has no beginning or end of days. The phrase is used four times in The Revelation (Rev. 1:8; Rev. 1:11; Rev. 21:6; and Rev. 22:13). The alphabet is an apt symbol of Jesus, the eternal Word. Nothing can be written without using an alphabet, and no one can be saved without receiving Jesus as Saviour.

The Place of John's Vision

9 I John, who also am your brother,

and companion in tribulation, and in the kingdom and patience of Jesus Christ, who <u>was in the isle that is called Patmos, for the word of God, and for the testimony of Jesus Christ.</u>

The Apostle John was exiled on the barren, lonely Isle of Patmos by Domitian about A.D. 95. Patmos is in the Aegean Sea, twenty miles from the nearest land. John's only crime was being faithful to the Word of God and the testimony of Jesus Christ. For that he had been banished.

John in the Spirit

10 <u>I was in the Spirit on the Lord's day,</u> and heard behind me a great voice, as of a trumpet.

John was in the Spirit on the Lord's Day. He could have been feeling sorry for himself. He had been faithful in the Lord's service, and for that he had been banished to this lonely island. He could not go to church, and he had no opportunity to preach. He could have spent the day pouting, but instead he was in the Spirit. He was having a good time of fellowship with the Lord, and, though he did not know it, he was about to begin his greatest ministry. If he had not been in the Spirit he would have missed the marvelous revelations the Lord was about to give him, and he would never have written The Revelation.

John's Commission to Write

11 Saying, I am Alpha and Omega, the first and the last: and, <u>What thou seest, write in a book, and send it unto the seven churches which are in Asia;</u> unto Ephesus, and unto Smyrna, and unto Pergamos, and unto Thyatira, and unto Sardis, and unto Philadelphia, and unto Laodicea.

John was commissioned to write letters to seven churches in Asia. This was not Asia Major but Asia Minor, and it did not include all of Asia Minor. It was only the western end of Asia Minor.

The seven churches that were to receive letters were not the only churches in Asia Minor. Three other churches in the region are mentioned in the New Testament, Colossae (Col. 1:2), Hierapolis (Col. 4:13), and Troas (Acts 20:6, 7). The seven churches that were to receive letters were selected and arranged in a sequence that would symbolize the church age, beginning with the church at Ephesus and ending with the churches of Philadelphia and Laodicea.

The letters John wrote should be viewed in four ways:

1. They contained messages for the churches that received them.

2. They contain truth for churches in all ages.

3. They contain truth for every believer.

4. They picture church history from the days of the apostles to the end of the age.

The seven churches represent the entire church age. Scholars who take this view differ slightly regarding the period of history that each church represents, but they agree that they picture the church age.

The late Dr. M. R. De Haan, in his book entitled, *Revelation,* published by Zondervan Publishing House in 1946, gives a good estimate of the dates represented by each of the seven churches. A paraphrase of what he wrote follows.

Ephesus was the church of the 1st century. Smyrna represents the church of the 2nd and 3rd centuries. Pergamos represents the church from about 312 A.D. to 500 A.D. Thyatira represents the church from the Dark Ages to the 16th century. Sardis was the church of the Renaissance and the Reformation. Philadelphia was the church in the revival of the 19th century. Laodicea will be the apostate church of the end-time.

Clarence Larkin, in his book, *The Book of Revelation*, takes the same view but differs regarding some of the dates. He wrote that the church of Ephesus covered the period from A.D. 70 to A.D. 170. He believed that the church of Smyrna represented the period of persecution from A.D. 170 to A.D. 312. He believed that Pergamos represented the period of history from A.D. 312 to A.D. 606. Thyatira he placed at A.D. 606 to A.D. 1520, Sardis at 1520 A.D. to about 1750 A.D. Philadelphia at 1750 A.D. to 1900 A.D.

Clarence Larkin served the Lord in the early nineteen hundreds. He believed that the church of Laodicea was a fair representative of the church of his day, and that it would be the only church that would continue until the rapture.

I differ with him and others who held the same position in one respect. I do not believe that the church of Laodicea will be the only end-time church. These men believe that all churches will be apostate at the time of the rapture. This cannot be, for Jesus said that the gates of hell will not prevail against the church (Matt. 16:18). He will find faith on the earth when He comes (Luke 18:8).

There will be apostate churches when Jesus returns, but there will also be Bible-preaching, soul-winning churches. The church of Philadelphia is a type of the true church of the last days. It was a Bible-believing, Christ-honoring church, and Jesus promised to set before it an open door to preach the Gospel. Philadelphian churches will coexist with the apostate Laodicean churches of the last days.

The liberal churches of our day will not amend their ways. They will continue to deny the truth of the Word of God. They will continue to deny the virgin birth and the resurrection of Jesus from the dead. They will continue to be little more than social clubs, with Christ outside until the rapture and beyond.

True churches will also continue, and the saved people in their membership will be raptured when Jesus comes for His bride. If only apostate churches should remain at the end of the age, there would be few believers for Jesus to rapture. It is evident that Bible-believing, soul-winning churches will continue to do the Lord's work until He comes again.

John's Vision of the Glorified Lord

12 And I turned to see the voice that spake with me. And being turned, I saw seven <u>golden candlesticks;</u>

13 And in the midst of the seven candlesticks one like unto the Son of man, <u>clothed with a garment down to the foot,</u> and <u>girt about the paps with a golden girdle.</u>

14 His head and his <u>hairs were white like wool, as white as snow;</u> and his eyes were as a flame of fire;

15 And <u>his feet like unto fine brass,</u>

as if they burned in a furnace; and <u>his</u>
<u>voice as the sound of many waters.</u>

John saw Jesus in the midst of seven golden candlesticks. The candlesticks are mentioned in verses 12 and 13, but it is not until verse 20 that their meaning is explained. It is sufficient to say here that John saw the risen, glorified Saviour standing in the midst of the candlesticks. A description of the Lord as John saw Him follows.

1. The Lord's robe

On the cross Jesus was stripped of His garments, and soldiers gambled for his robe. Now John saw the Lord fully clothed with a robe down to His feet.

2. The Lord's golden girdle

The golden girdle about the paps (breast) of the Lord was a sign of authority. Jesus is Lord of lords and King of kings.

3. The Lord's hair

The white hair of the glorified Lord tells us that He is the ancient of days described by the prophet, Daniel. Daniel wrote,

I beheld till the thrones were cast
down, and the Ancient of days did sit,
<u>whose garment was white as snow, and</u>
<u>the hair of his head like the pure wool:</u>
his throne was like the fiery flame, and
his wheels as burning fire (Dan. 7:9).

4. The Lord's eyes

The Lord's eyes were as a flame of fire. His eyes never appeared like that when He was on earth. Doubtless His eyes were stern when He rebuked the pharisees, but they did not look like burning fire. The Lord's eyes looking like flaming fire suggest the fire of judgment that will accompany His Second Coming.

5. The Lord's feet

The Lord's feet looked like brass. Brass is a symbol of judgment. When Moses lifted up the brazen serpent in the wilderness, it was a type of sin judged on the cross (Num. 21:8; John 3:14). Further, the brazen altar by the door of the tabernacle was called the altar of burnt offerings (Ex. 30:28). As a type of the cross it symbolized judgment. In His Second Coming, Christ will come to judge the world, and He will smite the nations and tread the winepress of fierceness of the wrath of God (Rev. 19:15).

6. The Lord's voice

The Lord's voice was like the sound of rushing water that drowns out all other sounds. When Jesus comes in judgment, He will speak with such authority that all other voices will be silenced.

7. The Two-edged sword

Verse 16 also tells us that a two-edged sword proceeded out of the mouth of the Lord. The Word of God is compared to a two-edged sword

in Hebrews 4:12. When Christ returns His words
will be like a two-edged sword. By His words
He will judge and condemn the wicked.

  8. The Lord's countenance
  Verse 16 tells us that Christ's countenance
was like the shining sun. That speaks of His glory.
Revelation 21:23 says that the glory of God will
be the light of the New Jerusalem.

The Meaning of the Seven Stars

*16 And he had in his right hand
seven stars; and out of his mouth went
a sharp twoedged sword: and his countenance was as the sun shineth in his
strength.*

Symbols used in The Revelation that are not
found elsewhere in the Bible are explained. The
meaning of the seven stars is given in verse 20.

The Glorious Presence of the Lord

*17 And when I saw him, I fell at his
feet as dead. And he laid his right hand
upon me, saying unto me, Fear not; I
am the first and the last:*

The Lord was so glorious that John fell at
His feet as if he were dead. Ezekiel had a similar
experience. He saw the Lord in a vision and fell
upon his face (Ezek. 1:28). Daniel had a vision
of the Lord and said, . . . *there remaineth no
strength in me (Dan. 10:8).* Saul of Tarsus fell to

the ground blinded by the vision of the Lord that he saw on his way to Damascus (Acts 9:3, 4). Our Lord is glorious beyond description.

The Keys of Death and Hell

18 I am he that liveth, and was dead; and, behold, I am alive for evermore, Amen; and have the keys of hell and of death.

Verse 18 gives us cause for rejoicing. The things men fear most are death and hell. Jesus was dead, but He is alive, and because He lives we shall live also. He has conquered death, and He has the keys of death and of hell. Paul has told us that the sting of death is gone (1 Cor. 15:55), and Jesus has told us that we will never be condemned (John 5:24). Death cannot hold us, and hell cannot claim us.

The Threefold Division of the Book

19 Write the things which thou hast seen, and the things which are, and the things which shall be hereafter;

Verse 19 is a key verse. It gives a threefold division of what John was told to write.

1. He was told to write about what he had seen (past tense).

2. He was told to write about the things that

now exist (present tense).

3. He was told to write about things that are yet to come (future tense).

In chapter 1, John wrote about his vision of the Lord. In chapters 2 and 3, he wrote about the churches that represent the church age. Then, beginning in chapter 4 and following, he wrote about the things that will occur after the rapture.

The Mystery of the Stars and Candlesticks

20 The <u>mystery of the seven stars</u> which thou sawest in my right hand, and <u>the seven golden candlesticks. The seven stars are the angels of the seven churches</u>: and <u>the seven candlesticks which thou sawest are the seven churches.</u>

In verse 20, as he often does, John writes about something he has mentioned previously. He wrote about the candlesticks in verse 12 and about the seven stars in verse 16. Now he tells the meaning of the stars and the candlesticks.

The word translated stars is sometimes translated messengers. That is a logical translation. These letters were to be read to the churches, and the logical persons to read them would not have been angels. Most likely the letters were read by the pastors of the churches that received them or by the messengers that delivered them.

The verse tells us that the golden candlesticks symbolize the churches. As gold is precious in the sight of men, churches are precious to our Lord. He loved the church and gave Himself for it (Eph. 5:25).

Candlesticks do not give light. They are designed to hold a candle that gives light. Churches do not give light, but they can let Jesus shine through them. That is also true of individual believers. In the sermon on the mount Jesus said,

Let your light so shine before men, that they may see your good works, and glorify your Father which is in heaven (Matt. 5:16).

Chapter 2

Jesus Walk in the Churches

*I*n verse 13 of chapter 1, John saw Jesus standing in the midst of seven golden candlesticks (churches). In chapter 2, verse 1, he saw Jesus walking in the midst of the candlesticks. Jesus has walked in His churches through the centuries, and He continues to walk in His churches today.

1. His walk is a walk of observation. Jesus observes all that is happening in every one of the churches.

2. His walk is a walk of commendation. He commends all that is good in the churches.

3. His walk is a walk of condemnation. He condemns that which is false and that which is sinful.

4. His walk is a walk of exhortation. He tells every church what to do.

5. His walk in the churches shows His de-

sire to communicate with His people. To every church He said, *"He that hath an ear, let him hear what the Spirit saith unto the churches. . . . "*

The still, small voice of the Spirit of God can only be heard by a spiritual ear. The text suggests that only part of God's people have spiritual hearing, and those who do have only one spiritual ear. By way of our spiritual ear the Holy Spirit speaks to us. Our spirit relays the message to our soul, and the soul has the task of communicating the message to a mind that is often tuned in on the world. That makes it difficult for us to hear what the Spirit is saying to us.

Jesus exhorted every church to listen to the leading of the Spirit. The admonition is given to the churches seven times in chapters 2 and 3, and it is given again in Revelation 13:9. That time it is given to those who have not received the mark of the beast. They will need to be led by the Spirit instead of following the inclinations of the flesh.

Only the children of God have the privilege of being led by the Spirit. *"For as many as are led by the Spirit of God, they are the sons of God"* *(Rom. 8:14).* The oft-repeated command to listen to what the Spirit has to say should cause us to take time to shut out the world and seek the leading of the Lord.

The Walk of Observation
Contents of Chapter 2

I. The letter to the church at Ephesus (verses 1-7)
  1. The walk of observation (verses 1-3)
  2. The walk of condemnation (verse 4)
  3. The walk of exhortation (verse 5)
  4. The sect of the Nicolaitanes (verse 6)
  5. The first admonition to hear the Spirit (verse 7)

II. The letter to the church of Smyrna (verses 8-11)
  1. The walk of observation (verses 8, 9)
  2. The walk of exhortation (verse 10)
  3. Second admonition to hear the Spirit (verse 11)

III. The letter to the church in Pergamos (verses 12-17)
  1. The walk of observation (verses 12, 13)
  2. The walk of condemnation (verses 14, 15)
  3. The walk of exhortation (verse 16)
  3. Third admonition to hear the Spirit (verse 17)

IV. The letter to the church of Thyatira (verses 18-29)
  1. Walk of observation (verses 18, 19)
  2. The walk of condemnation (verses 20-23)
  3. Mercy to the faithful (verses 24, 25)
  4. The promise of future victory (verses 26-28)
  5. Fourth admonition to hear the Spirit (verse 29)

1 Unto the angel of the church of Ephesus write; <u>These things saith he that holdeth the seven stars in his right hand, who walketh in the midst of the seven golden candlesticks;</u>

2 <u>I know thy works,</u> and thy labour, and thy patience, and how thou canst not bear them which are evil: and thou hast tried them which say they are

apostles, and are not, and hast found them liars:
    3 And hast borne, and hast patience, and for my name's sake hast laboured, and hast not fainted.

The salutation to the church at Ephesus gives us a wonderful picture of our Lord walking in His churches and holding the pastors in His right hand. It shows His concern about what happens to His churches and to the pastors of the churches. Even when the disciples at Jerusalem were scattered by persecution, we are told in Acts 11:21 that the hand of the Lord was with them. He continued to bless and use them, and great numbers of people were converted.

Jesus knew all about this church, as He does about every church, and He recognized everything that was good first. He does the same today. Nothing that we do in the Lord's service goes unnoticed. Some people may not appreciate what we are doing in the Lord's work, but Jesus does. He has even promised to reward those who give a cup of water in his name (Matt. 10:42).

The Walk of Condemnation

4 Nevertheless <u>I have somewhat against thee, because thou hast left thy first love.</u>

The church at Ephesus was a good, moral,

decent church. The people had committed no big sins, but they were backslidden in heart. After commending them for their works and their patience, Jesus condemned them for leaving their first love.

The Walk of Exhortation

5 Remember therefore from whence thou art fallen, and repent, and do the first works; or else I will come unto thee quickly, and will remove thy candlestick out of his place, except thou repent.

Jesus warned the church at Ephesus that if they did not repent He would remove their candlestick out of its place. That means that He would take away their ability to give light. A church without light is a church without power. There are churches today that have had their light removed. They no longer give light, and they no longer win souls. Over the door of such churches should be written, the word, "Ichabod," the glory has departed (1 Sam. 4:21).

The Sect of the Nicolaitanes

6 But this thou hast, that thou hatest the deeds of the Nicolaitanes, which I also hate.

There is no apparent history of the sect of the Nicolaitanes, but Scofield has a good comment about them on page 1332 of the old Scofield Bible. He wrote in part: "From nikao, to conquer, and laos, the people." Even in the early days of the church there were those who wanted to usurp authority over God's people. That was not pleasing to God in that day, and it is not pleasing to Him today.

The First Admonition to Hear the Spirit

7 He that hath an ear, let him hear what the Spirit saith unto the churches; To him that overcometh will I give to eat of the tree of life, which is in the midst of the paradise of God.

In each of the letters to the seven churches our Lord's last admonition was that they should listen to the leading of the Spirit. Being led by the Holy Spirit was needed in the first century, and it is needed today. Following the leading of God's Spirit will solve problems, meet needs, and kindle revival fires.

The Letter to the Church of Smyrna
The Walk of Observation

8 And unto the angel of the church in Smyrna write; These things saith the first and the last, which was dead, and is alive;

9 I know thy works, and tribulation, and poverty, (but thou art rich) and I know the blasphemy of them which say they are Jews, and are not, but are the synagogue of Satan.

Jesus commended the church at Smyrna for their faithful works under difficult circumstances, but He did not overlook false professors. He knew that the people were poor, but He told them that they were rich. They were poor in worldly possessions, but they possessed spiritual riches. On the other hand, Jesus condemned the church of Laodicea for being rich in worldly possessions and poor in spiritual riches.

The Walk of Exhortation

10 <u>Fear none of those things which thou shalt suffer:</u> behold, the devil shall cast some of you into prison, that ye may be tried; and ye shall have tribulation ten days: <u>be thou faithful unto death, and I will give thee a crown of life.</u>

Jesus told the church of Smyrna not to fear the persecution it was to suffer. Its members were to be cast into prison and tried for ten days. Jesus told them to be faithful unto death, and He would give them a crown of life.

When the Romans were in power they gave a crown of death to a soldier who died in battle. At his funeral, a high ranking officer would place an olive wreath on his brow. It was called the crown of death. That was a high honor, but it did not compare to the crown of life that the Lord will give to those who die in His service. The slain Roman soldier could only wear a crown of death in his casket. The crown of life that Christ will give will be worn in Heaven.

The ten days of tribulation may represent the ten periods of persecution that the church was to suffer, beginning under Nero about A.D. 64 and ending under Diocletian A.D. 310 Polycarp was martyred during that time. He was pastor in Smyrna about A.D. 115 It is said that the Apostle John led him to Christ when he was a small boy.

Second Admonition to Hear the Spirit

11 He that hath an ear, let him hear what the Spirit saith unto the churches; He that overcometh shall not be hurt of the second death.

The Letter to the Church in Pergamos
The Walk of Observation

12 And to the angel of the church in Pergamos write; These things saith he which hath the sharp sword with two edges;

13 I know thy works, and where thou dwellest, even where Satan's seat is: and thou holdest fast my name, and hast not denied my faith, even in those days wherein Antipas was my faithful martyr, who was slain among you, where Satan dwelleth.

The church in Pergamos had been faithful under difficult circumstances, but it had some serious problems. Perhaps that is why Jesus warned them in verse 12 that He had a sharp sword with two edges. In verse 16 He told them that if they did not repent He would fight against them with the sword of His mouth.

In verse 13 Jesus told the church that He knew they had been faithful, even when one of their number had been martyred, and He knew that they were located in a wicked, idolatrous city that was the dwelling place of Satan. The city of Pergamos had built splendid temples to Jupiter, Athena, Apollo, and AEsculapius. The emblem of AEsculapius was a serpent, hence the term, Satan's seat.

The Walk of Condemnation

14 But I have a few things against thee, because thou hast there them that hold the doctrine of Balaam, who taught Balac to cast a stumblingblock before the children of Israel, to eat things sacrificed unto idols, and to commit fornication.

15 So hast thou also them that hold the doctrine of the Nicolaitanes, which thing I hate.

Jesus condemned this church for holding the doctrine of Balaam. Balaam tried to serve God while disobeying Him for personal gain. Jude wrote of those who followed the way of Balaam for reward (Jude 11). Peter wrote of those who went after the way of Balaam for the wages of unrighteousness (2 Pet. 2:15). The church at Pergamos was condemned for putting personal gain ahead of serving God.

The Walk of Exhortation

16 <u>Repent; or else</u> I will come unto thee quickly, and will fight against them with the sword of my mouth.

Jesus warned the church of Pergamos to repent or face judgment. Five of the seven churches were told to repent. Only Smyrna, the church under persecution, and Philadelphia, the faithful church of the open door, were not told to repent.

The church at Pergamos was told to repent, but overcomers in their number were promised hidden manna. The manna that the children of Israel ate in the wilderness was called bread from Heaven. Jesus is the true bread from Heaven, and He is only hidden to those who are blinded by Satan.

Then Jesus said unto them, Verily, verily, I say unto you, Moses gave you not that bread from heaven; but my Father giveth you the true bread from heaven (John 6:32).

Third Admonition to Hear the Spirit

17 He that hath an ear, let him hear

what the Spirit saith unto the churches;
To him that overcometh will I give to eat
of the hidden manna, and will give him
a white stone, and in the stone a new
name written, which no man knoweth
saving he that receiveth it.

There is little agreement among Bible commentaries about the meaning of the white stone containing the new name that Jesus promised to overcomers. It is sufficient to say that the new name is for those who have a new birth, a new nature, a new life, and a new home.

The Letter to the Church of Thyatira
The Walk of Observation

18 And unto the angel of the church
in Thyatira write; These things saith the
Son of God, who hath his eyes like unto
a flame of fire, and his feet are like fine
brass;
19 I know thy works, and charity,
and service, and faith, and thy patience,
and thy works; and the last to be more
than the first.

Jesus begins the letter to the church at Thyatira by reminding them that He has all-seeing eyes and feet of judgment. Then He commends them for their works, their love, their service, their faith, and their patience. This church had some problems, but, even so, Jesus was pleased with the work they were doing.

The Walk of Condemnation

20 Notwithstanding I have a few things against thee, because thou sufferest that woman Jezebel, which calleth herself a prophetess, to teach and to seduce my servants to commit fornication, and to eat things sacrificed unto idols.

21 And I gave her space to repent of her fornication; and she repented not.

22 Behold, I will cast her into a bed, and them that commit adultery with her into great tribulation, except they repent of their deeds.

23 And I will kill her children with death; and all the churches shall know that I am he which searcheth the reins and hearts: and I will give unto every one of you according to your works.

Much was wrong with the church at Thyatira. There was a woman in the membership that Jesus called *that woman, Jezebel.* Her conduct must have reminded the Lord of the Jezebel of the Old Testament who was the pagan daughter of Ethbaal, king of Zidon (1 Kings 16:31). That Jezebel was married to Ahab, the seventh king of the northern kingdom of Israel. She sought to kill all the true prophets of Jehovah and make Israel a pagan nation. She built heathen temples and supported 450 prophets of Baal. This woman, Jezebel, who called herself a prophetess, must have been wicked indeed. Yet the church suffered her to teach and to seduce God's servants and lead them into immoral practices. That was an attempt by Satan to destroy the church from within. He often tries to do the same today.

In spite of Jezebel's wickedness, Jesus gave her space to repent, but He promised severe punishment to her and those who sinned with her if they did not repent.

Mercy to the Faithful

24 But unto you I say, and unto the rest in Thyatira, <u>as many as have not this doctrine, and which have not known the depths of Satan, as they speak; I will put upon you none other burden.</u>

25 But that which ye have already hold fast till I come.

The church of Thyatira was a terribly divided church. Some of the members were sold out to Satan, and others were faithful to the Lord. Jesus promised the faithful ones that He would put upon them no other burden, and He admonished them to remain faithful until His Second Coming.

The Promise of Future Victory

26 And he that overcometh, and keepeth my works unto the end, to him will I give power over the nations:

27 And he shall rule them with a rod of iron; as the vessels of a potter shall they be broken to shivers: even as I received of my Father.

28 And I will give him the morning star.

Verses 26 through 28 look forward to the kingdom when Jesus will reign, and His bride will inherit the earth and reign with Him. He will give the morning star to the faithful. Jesus is the morning star (Rev. 22:16). That means that He will give Himself to those who serve Him faithfully.

The Fourth Admonition to Hear the Spirit

29 He that hath an ear, let him hear what the Spirit saith unto the churches.

Chapter 3

Introduction to Chapter 3

*C*hapter 3 tells of Jesus' continued walk in the churches. His letters to Sardis, Philadelphia, and Laodicea shows again that He knows all about His churches and is concerned about their welfare.

He also knows all about His pastors and is ready to empower them, guide them, and use them when they walk in His perfect will.

He is also concerned about every individual. Even though the church of Laodicea had shut Him out, He stood at the door knocking and offering to come in to anyone who would open the door to Him.

Contents of Chapter 3

I. The letter to the church at Sardis (verses 1-6)
   1. Walk of observation and condemnation (verse 1)
   2. The walk of exhortation (verses 2, 3)
   3. A message to the faithful (verses 4, 5)
   4. Fifth admonition to be led by the Spirit (verse 6)

II. The letter to the church of Philadelphia (verses 7-13)
1. The walk of observation (verses 7-9)
2. The walk of commendation (verses 10-12)
3. Sixth admonition to be led by the Spirit (verse 13)

III. The letter to the church at Laodicea (verses 14-22)
1. The walk of observation (verses 14, 15)
2. The walk of condemnation (verses 16, 17)
3. The walk of exhortation (verses 18, 19)
4. Jesus knocking at the church door (verses 20, 21)
5. Seventh admonition to be led by the Spirit (verse 22)

The Letter to the Church in Sardis
The Walk of Observation and Commendation

1 And unto the angel of the church in Sardis write; These things saith he that hath the seven Spirits of God, and the seven stars; I know thy works, that thou hast a name that thou livest, and art dead.

Jesus reminds the church in Sardis that He has the seven Spirits of God and the seven stars. As we have already noted, the stars are pastors, and the seven Spirits of God are eyes that are sent into all the world (Rev. 5:6).

The condemnation of the church in Sardis is contained in the brief statement, *thou hast a name that thou livest, and art dead.* There is nothing more tragic than a dead church that has only the name of being alive.

The Walk of Exhortation
2 Be watchful, and strengthen the

*things which remain, that are ready to
die: for I have not found thy works perfect before God.*

*3 Remember therefore how thou
hast received and heard, and hold fast,
and repent. If therefore thou shalt not
watch, I will come on thee as a thief,
and thou shalt not know what hour I will
come upon thee.*

The church in Sardis was dead, but the
Lord's exhortation in verses 2 and 3 shows His
patience and His desire to work with the people
in the church who were not dead.

Jesus told the church of Ephesus to remember from where they had fallen and repent. He
commanded those who were spiritually alive in
this church to hold fast and repent. That indicates that even those who were alive were backslidden.

There are times when people need to repent.
Lost people need to repent and believe for salvation. Backsliders need to repent and confess
their sins for forgiveness, and others need to repent because of their shortcomings in the Lord's
service.

A Message to the Faithful

*4 Thou hast a few names even in
Sardis which have not defiled their garments; and they shall walk with me in
white: for they are worthy.*

*5 <u>He that overcometh, the same
shall be clothed in white raiment;</u> and I
will not blot out his name out of the book
of life, but I <u>will confess his name before my Father, and before his angels.</u>*

The life that remained in the dead church at Sardis consisted of a few godly members. Jesus recognized them and promised to reward them.

There are saved people in dead churches today, and they lose much because of that affiliation. They miss the fellowship they could have in vibrant, spiritual churches, and they waste their time, their testimonies, and their money in churches that are accomplishing little in the Lord's work.

Saved people in dead churches have much to overcome. The atmosphere and influence of a dead church robs them of joy and victory and keeps them from being effective in the Lord's service. But that does not keep them from being saved. Those who have received Jesus as Saviour are saved by grace, and the Lord loves them in spite of their having membership in dead churches. He promises the saved people in Sardis that He will confess their names before His Father and His angels.

The Fifth Admonition to be Led by the Spirit

*6 He that hath an ear, let him hear
what the Spirit saith unto the churches.*

The Church of Philadelphia
The Walk of Observation

7 And to the angel of the church in Philadelphia write; These things saith he that is holy, he that is true, he that hath the key of David, <u>he that openeth, and no man shutteth; and shutteth, and no man openeth;</u>

8 I know thy works: behold, <u>I have set before thee an open door, and no man can shut it: for thou hast a little strength, and hast kept my word, and hast not denied my name.</u>

9 Behold, <u>I will make them of the synagogue of Satan, which say they are Jews, and are not, but do lie;</u> behold, <u>I will make them to come and worship before thy feet, and to know that I have loved thee.</u>

As stated in chapter 1, the church of Philadelphia is a type of the true churches that will be on earth at the end of the age. Liberal churches, typified by the church of Laodicea, will coexist with them and will be on earth when Jesus comes to rapture His own.

Satan and all his demons cannot stop the ministry of a faithful church. That was true in ages past. It is true today, and it will be true until the end of the age. Jesus has all power in Heaven and on earth, and He has promised to be with His servants until the end of the age (Matt. 28:18, 20).

The Bible tells us that the church in Philadelphia had an open door set before it. There were good reasons for Jesus to set an open door before this church. For the same reasons, churches of the Philadelphian mold will have open doors set before them to preach the gospel until the end of the age. The reasons for the open door follow:

1. The church of Philadelphia had a little strength.

2. It was faithful to the Word of God.

3. It did not deny the name of the Lord Jesus Christ.

A church does not have to be large or strong to be faithful and useful. God will bless any church that meets the conditions for His blessings. The church at Philadelphia was a Bible-centered church. The people believed, taught, and practiced the Word of God, and they had not denied the threefold name of the Lord Jesus Christ. They had believed in Him as Jesus, the virgin-born Son of God. They had served Him as the Lord of Glory, and they had honored Him as Christ, the soon-coming King.

When the letter to the church of Philadelphia was written there were false religions and false professors, but that did not keep the church from being faithful. There are liberal churches and false cults in the world today. They will remain until the Lord comes again, but that will not keep true believers from being faithful to the Lord and His Word. There are more Christ honoring, Bible-believing, soul-winning churches on earth today than we can count, and there will be true churches on earth until the Lord translates them to Heaven.

Verse 9 looks forward to the time when Christ will come again and the church will reign with Him. Then He will condemn false professors and make them come and worship before the feet of true believers.

The Walk of Commendation

10 Because thou hast kept the word of my patience, I also will keep thee from the hour of temptation, which shall come upon all the world, to try them that dwell upon the earth.

11 Behold, I come quickly: hold that fast which thou hast, that no man take thy crown.

12 Him that overcometh will I make a pillar in the temple of my God, and he shall go no more out: and I will write upon him the name of my God, and the name of the city of my God, which is new

Jerusalem, which cometh down out of heaven from my God: and I will write upon him my new name.

The promise that the church of Philadelphia would not have to go through the hour of temptation had an application in that day. It also looked forward to the end-time tribulation. Saved people will escape the tribulation by being raptured before it begins. There follows in verse 11 the admonition to be faithful because Jesus will soon come again.

Verse 12 looks forward to the Second Coming of Christ. Those who have remained faithful will be made pillars in the temple of God, and they will be given the name of God, the name of the city of God, and the Lord's new name. There will not only be a new name, there will be a new address. The new address will be, The New Jerusalem.

God likes names. He had Adam to name all the animals He had created. God named the stars, and He knows them all by name (Psa. 147:4). God himself has many names. God often changes people's names to reflect changes in their lifestyle. He changed Abram's name to Abraham. He changed Sarai's name to Sara, and He changed Jacob's name to Israel.

Jesus also likes names. He changed Simon

Peter's name to Cephas, and it is not surprising that He will give new names to His faithful servants when He translates them to Heaven.

The Sixth Admonition to be Led by the Spirit

13 He that hath an ear, let him hear what the Spirit saith unto the churches.

The Letter to the Church of Laodicea
The Walk of Observation

14 And unto the angel of the church of the Laodiceans write; These things saith the Amen, the faithful and true witness, the beginning of the creation of God;

15 <u>I know thy works, that thou art neither cold nor hot: I would thou wert cold or hot.</u>

Jesus begins the letter to the church of Laodicea by saying, *"I know thy works."* He is not pleased with the works of this church. He found this church lukewarm and disgusting. There was no walk of commendation for this church, for it was a church of the world.

The members thought of their church as being rich and needing nothing, but in the Lord's sight it was wretched, miserable, poor, blind, and naked. Even worse, Jesus was outside the door of the church knocking for an entrance to anyone who would open the door for Him.

The Walk of Condemnation

16 <u>So then because thou art luke-warm, and neither cold nor hot, I will spue thee out of my mouth.</u>

17 Because thou sayest, I am rich, and increased with goods, and have need of nothing; <u>and knowest not that thou art wretched, and miserable, and poor, and blind, and naked:</u>

Jesus condemned the church of Laodicea for being puffed up, boastful of riches, and spiritually ignorant. Their possessions were in the world, and their interests were of the world. They had made no preparation to go to Heaven, and they had laid up no treasures there.

The Walk of Exhortation

18 <u>I counsel thee to buy of me gold tried in the fire, that thou mayest be rich;</u> and white raiment, that thou mayest be clothed, and that the shame of thy nakedness do not appear; and anoint thine eyes with eyesalve, that thou mayest see.

19 <u>As many as I love, I rebuke and chasten: be zealous therefore, and repent.</u>

The members of the church of Laodicea were spiritually blind. They did not realize that they were poor, blind, and naked, and they did not know that they were no more than a social club with Jesus shut on the outside. Churches like the Laodicean church will increase in number as we approach the end of the age.

It appears that there will be some saved people in such end-time churches, for Jesus counseled them to repent and buy of Him gold, that can only be obtained by going through the fire of trial, and white raiment that comes with the new birth. One of the surprises we will have when we get to Heaven will be seeing people from liberal churches who were saved in spite of what the church they belonged to taught and practiced.

Jesus Knocking at the Door

20 Behold, I stand at the door, and knock: if any man hear my voice, and open the door, I will come in to him, and will sup with him, and he with me.

21 To him that overcometh will I grant to sit with me in my throne, even as I also overcame, and am set down with my Father in his throne.

There can be no better picture of our Lord's compassion and concern for people in worldly churches than we find here. He is shut out of the church, but He stands at the door knocking, ready to come in to anyone who will open the door for Him. The Lord could not fellowship with this church, but He was eager to fellowship with anyone who would open the door and let Him in. Even in the disgusting, Christ-rejecting church of Laodicea, overcoming believers were promised a home in Heaven.

Seventh Admonition to be Led by the Spirit

22 _He that hath an ear, let him hear what the Spirit saith unto the churches._

It is interesting that even in the corrupt church of Laodicea Jesus appeals to anyone with a spiritual ear to hear what the Spirit is saying to the churches.

Chapter 4

Introduction to Chapter 4

*C*hapter 4 opens with the words *"After this."* That means after the church age has ended. The chapter then pictures the rapture and events that will follow in Heaven.

John saw a door open in Heaven and heard again the trumpetlike voice he had heard when he saw Christ glorified in chapter 1. This time the voice said, *"Come up hither,"* and he was transported to Heaven. John being removed from the earthly scene is a picture of what will happen to all the children of God when Jesus comes for His church.

In Heaven John was safe from the judgments of the tribulation. After the rapture the church will be safe from the tribulation. The prophet Isaiah wrote of the tribulation and of the door of safety for the saved as follows:

> *Come, my people, enter thou into thy chambers, and shut thy doors about*

thee: hide thyself as it were for a little moment, until the indignation be overpast (Isa. 26:20).

The indignation that Isaiah wrote about in the Old Testament is the equivalent of the tribulation in the New Testament. Both tribulation and indignation speak of the wrath of God.

The trumpetlike voice of the Lord is an additional evidence that this chapter pictures the rapture. In Paul's description of the rapture he also wrote of that trumpetlike voice.

For the Lord himself shall descend from heaven with a shout, with the voice of the archangel, and <u>with the trump</u> <u>of God:</u> and the dead in Christ shall rise first (1 Thess. 4:16).

Contents of Chapter 4

1. John translated to Heaven (verse 1)
2. John's first vision in Heaven (verses 2, 3)
3. The twenty-four elders around the throne (verse 4)
4. The lamps of fire and sea of glass (verses 5, 6)
5. The four beasts (verses 7-9)
6. The elders worship God (verses 10, 11)

John Translated to Heaven

1 <u>After this</u> I looked, and, <u>behold, a door was opened in heaven: and the first voice which I heard was as it were of a trumpet talking with me; which said, Come up hither,</u> and <u>I will shew thee</u>

things which must be hereafter.

After John was translated to Heaven his visions were about things that will happen after the church is raptured. He did not mention the church again until chapter 19. In that chapter the church reappears as the bride of Christ. The lack of any mention of the church between chapter 3 and chapter 19 is an evidence that this chapter pictures the rapture.

John's First Vision in Heaven

2 And *immediately I was in the* *spirit: and, behold, a throne was set in* *heaven, and one sat on the throne.*

3 And he that sat was to look upon like *a jasper and a sardine stone:* *and there was* *a rainbow round about the* *throne, in sight like unto an emerald.*

John's first vision after he was translated was of God seated on His throne. Revelation 5:7 makes it clear that it was the Father. There we are told that the Lamb (Jesus) took the seven-sealed book from the One who sat on the throne.

Much of John's first vision in Heaven relates to the throne of God. The throne was encircled by an emerald rainbow. Twenty-four elders were seated around the throne. Seven lamps of fire were burning before the throne, and there was a sea of glass before the throne. Four beasts were in the midst of and around the throne. They were giving honor and thanks to God, and the twenty-four elders were worshiping and praising Him. This tells us that the first thing that will happen after the rapture will be a glorious time of worshiping and praising God.

The description of God tells us little beyond the fact that His appearance was like a jasper and a sardine stone. The jasper is clear and brilliant like a diamond, and the sardine stone is red like a ruby. The jasper speaks of the glory of God, and the sardine is a reminder of the blood of Christ.

The rainbow around the throne was green like an emerald. The emerald was the stone of the tribe of Juda. Jesus came from that tribe. The jasper, the sardine, and the emerald were three of the twelve stones in the breastplate that Old Testament priests wore when they ministered in the priest's office.

The rainbow around the throne speaks of judgment passed. A rainbow comes after a storm. The first mention of a rainbow in the Bible is in Genesis 9:13. After the flood God used the rainbow as a token that He would never again destroy the earth with a flood. The rainbow around the throne of God means that the storm of judgment has passed for those who have gone to Heaven in the rapture.

An earthly rainbow is a half circle. The rainbow around the throne of God was an unbroken circle. That means that judgment has forever passed for the raptured children of God.

The heavenly rainbow does not have the color of an earthly rainbow. An earthly rainbow is formed from the refracted light of the sun. The heavenly rainbow will be formed by the light of the glory of God.

John was not the only one to see a rainbow around the throne of God. Six hundred and ninety-one years before John was banished to Patmos, Ezekiel had a vision of a rainbow around God's throne. Following is a part of what Ezekiel saw.

And above the firmment that was over their heads was the likeness of a throne, as the appearance of a sapphire stone . . . And I saw as the colour of amber, as the appearance of fire round about within it, . . . As the appearance of the bow that is in the cloud in the day of rain, so was the appearance of the brightness round about. This was the appearance of the likeness of the glory of the LORD . . . (Ezek. 1:26, 27, 28.

The Twenty-four Elders Around the Throne

4 And round about the throne were four and twenty seats: and upon the seats I saw four and twenty elders sit-

ting, clothed in white raiment; and they
had on their heads crowns of gold.

There has been much speculation about what the four and twenty elders symbolize. They are not angels as some suppose, and they are not Jewish converts as others believe. They are the redeemed from all nations that have gone up in the rapture.

The church is now in Heaven, and it is represented by the twenty-four elders around the throne of God. The twenty-four elders are mentioned eleven additional times in The Revelation.

The twenty-four elders were wearing white raiment. White raiment indicates that they were blood-washed. In Revelation 5:9 we find the twenty-four elders singing a new song that says in part that the Lamb had redeemed them out of all nations by His blood.

The number twenty-four is the number of priesthood. In 1 Chr. 24 we are told that there were twenty-four divisions of the sons of Aaron, the priestly tribe. That reminds us that the raptured people of the church will be priests of God and Christ (Rev. 20:6).

The elders were wearing crowns of gold. That means that they were kings. Only the redeemed church can fit the picture of a royal, blood-washed priesthood.

Much is written in The Revelation about worship. After John passed through the door in Heaven he saw the elders cast their crowns before the throne of God and fall down to worship Him (Rev. 4:10). In Revelation 5:8 we find them falling down before the Lamb, and in verse 14 we read that they fell down and worshiped the One who lives for ever and ever. In Revelation 11:16 we are told that they fell upon their faces and worshiped God. Finally, in Revelation 19:4 we read:

> *And the four and twenty elders and the four beasts fell down and worshipped God that sat on the throne, saying, Amen; Alleluia.*

All of this is only the beginning of the worship, and praise, and glory that we will share after the rapture.

The Lamps of Fire and Sea of Glass

> *5 And out of the throne proceeded lightnings and thunderings and voices: and there were <u>seven lamps of fire burning before the throne, which are the seven spirits of God.</u>*
>
> *6 <u>And before the throne there was a sea of glass like unto crystal:</u> and in the midst of the throne, and round about the throne, were four beasts full of eyes be-*

fore and behind.

Verse 5 explains again that the seven lamps of fire before the throne are the seven Spirits of God. The meaning of the sea of glass is unclear, but it suggests tranquility. On earth the sea and the waves are always roaring (Luke 21:25), but the raptured saints will not be touched by raging storms of tossing waves.

The Four Beasts

7 And <u>the first beast was like a lion, and the second beast like a calf, and the third beast had a face as a man, and the fourth beast was like a flying eagle.</u>

8 And <u>the four beasts had each of them six wings about him; and they were full of eyes within: and they rest not day and night, saying, Holy, holy, holy, Lord God Almighty,</u> which was, and is, and is to come.

9 And when <u>those beasts give glory and honour and thanks to him that sat on the throne, who liveth for ever and ever.</u>

The four beasts mentioned in verse 6 are described as follows: the first beast was like a lion, the second beast was like a calf, the third beast had the face of a man, and the fourth beast was like a flying eagle. This description is obviously symbolic.

Scholars have long debated what the beasts symbolize. At least thirty suggestions have been made regarding the meaning of the beasts, and none of them shed any light on what they symbolize.

This much we can know. The word translated "beast" is (Zoon). In the original language it means "living creatures." A comparison of Revelation 4:8 with Isaiah's vision of seraphim in Isaiah 6:1-3 reveals that the living creatures in John's vision are the same as the seraphim in Isaiah's vision.

Seraphim are a high order of angels that serve near the throne of God. Their chief occupation appears to be praising God. In both references sited, the seraphim have six wings, and in both references they are praising God. In Isaiah's vision they were saying, . . . *Holy, holy, holy, is the LORD of hosts: the whole earth is full of his glory.*

In Revelation 4:8, they were saying, . . . *Holy, holy, holy, Lord God Almighty.*

Little more can be said about the four beasts other than the lion stands for courage, the calf for patience, the man for spirituality, and the eagle for heavenly flight.

The four beasts are always near the throne, and they never cease to worship and praise God.

In contrast, Satan, a fallen angel, tempted Jesus to worship him.

The Elders Worship God

10 The four and twenty elders fall down before him that sat on the throne, and worship him that liveth for ever and ever, and cast their crowns before the throne, saying.

11 Thou art worthy, O Lord, to receive glory and honour and power: for thou hast created all things, and for thy pleasure they are and were created.

Verses 10 and 11 give us another picture of the redeemed saints worshiping God after the rapture. In these verses the twenty-four elders fall before God, cast their crowns before the throne, and praise Him.

Verse 11 tells us that God is worthy to receive glory and honor because He is the creator of all things. Then we read that all things are created for His pleasure. That explains why God has created a universe too vast for man to explore or understand. He creates for His pleasure.

Creating is God's recreation. The beginning described in the first chapter of Genesis may describe only the beginning of our earth and solar system. For all we know, God may have been creating heavenly bodies for millions of years before that, and God may still be creating additional galaxies in the cosmos for His own pleasure.

We know that God will create in the future. We read that He will create a new Heaven and a new earth (Rev. 21:1). God is great and glorious. His power and glory are beyond our understanding.

Chapter 5

Introduction to Chapter 5

*C*hapter 5 opens with God on His throne holding a sealed book in His right hand. The book, in the form of a scroll, contained the title deed to the earth.

When the earth was created God owned it by right of creation (Lev. 25:23). He gave the earth to Adam and Eve, but they lost it when they sinned. Satan then took possession of the earth, and he has controlled it ever since.

When Satan tempted Jesus on the mountain, he offered to give Him all the kingdoms of the world in return for His worship (Matt. 4:8, 9). Jesus refused to worship Satan, but He did not question that Satan had control of the kingdoms of the world.

Satan still controls the kingdoms of the world. Witness the sin, the violence, the wars, and the rumors of war that are taking place in the world. All of these will continue as long as Satan is in control, and he will be in control until Jesus redeems the world.

Contents of Chapter 5

1. The seven-sealed book (verse 1)
2. The search for someone to break the seals (verses 2, 3)
3. John's cause for weeping (verse 4)
4. The One worthy to open the book (verses 5-7)
5. Rejoicing in Heaven (verses 8-10)
6. The angels rejoice (verses 11, 12)
7. Universal recognition of the Redeemer (verses 13, 14)

The Seven-sealed Book

1 And <u>I saw in the right hand of him that sat on the throne a book written within and on the backside, sealed with seven seals.</u>

The scroll in God's hand had writing on both sides, and it was sealed with seven seals. It contained the terms that had to be met to redeem the lost earth.

To understand the redemption of the earth we need to understand the law of the kinsman redeemer. God gave the children of Israel possession of the Promised Land, but they did not own the land. If a man decided to sell his possession because of poverty, he could only sell the right to possess it until the year of jubilee which came every fifty years. On the year of jubilee the land had to be returned to the family that had received it from God.

Under Levitical law, if a man sold his possession, a near kinsman who could meet the conditions required of a redeemer could redeem it

(Lev. 25:25). He had to be a kinsman. He had to have the price of the lost possession, and he had to be able to meet the terms of the contract.

When a scroll contained information not intended for the general public, such as a deed or contract, was rolled up and sealed, the terms of the contract could not be read until the seals were broken. Only general information contained on the outside of the scroll could be read. The breaking of each seal made it possible for part of the scroll to be unrolled and read.

The Search for Someone to Break the Seals

2 And I saw a strong angel proclaiming with a loud voice, <u>Who is worthy to open the book, and to loose the seals thereof?</u>

3 And <u>no man in heaven, nor in earth, neither under the earth, was able to open the book, neither to look thereon.</u>

A search was made to find someone who was worthy to break the seals and read the terms that had to be met to redeem the lost earth. The earth had been lost by sin, so the redeemer had to be someone who was without sin.

Verse 3 tells us that Heaven, earth, and hell were searched for a redeemer, but no one was found who was worthy to loose the seals and meet the terms of the contract. Those in hell are guilty, condemned sinners, so they are not worthy. Men on the earth, even the saved, are living in unredeemed bodies, and they are not worthy. Those in Heaven were saved by grace and have no merit of their own, so they are not worthy.

John's Cause for Weeping

4 <u>And I wept much,</u> because no man was found worthy to open and to read the book, neither to look thereon.

John understood what the breaking of the seals would accomplish. When no man was found worthy to open the book, he could not bear the thought of the world continuing in the control of Satan, and that caused him to shed many tears.

The redeeming of the earth would cause the curse to be lifted. Sin, sickness, sorrow, suffering, and death would be no more. Both religious Babylon and commercial Babylon would be judged. Antichrist would be destroyed. Satan would be cast into the lake of fire and brimstone, and the reign of everlasting righteousness would begin. If no one was found worthy to break the seals and look upon the book, all would be lost. But John soon had cause to dry his tears, for a redeemer was found!

The One Worthy to Open the Book

5 And one of the elders saith unto me, Weep not: behold, <u>the Lion of the tribe of Juda, the Root of David, hath</u>

prevailed to open the book, and to loose the seven seals thereof.

6 And I beheld, and, lo, in the midst of the throne and of the four beasts, and in the midst of the elders, stood a Lamb as it had been slain, having seven horns and seven eyes, which are the seven Spirits of God sent forth into all the earth.

7 And he came and took the book out of the right hand of him that sat upon the throne.

One of the elders told John to stop crying for, . . . *the Lion of the tribe of Juda, the Root of David, hath prevailed to open the book, and to loose the seven seals thereof.*

In verse 6 the Redeemer is pictured as a Lamb that had been slain and yet was standing. That speaks of the death and resurrection of Jesus. Only the slain Lamb of God was able to pay the sin debt, and only the risen Lord can redeem the world that is groaning under the curse of sin.

The Lamb John saw had seven horns and seven eyes. The seven horns are symbols of power. Seven is the number of completeness. That means that Jesus has all power. The seven eyes are the seven Spirits of God that will be sent forth into all the earth. This may symbolize God looking over the redeemed possession.

Rejoicing in Heaven

8 And <u>when he had taken the book, the four beasts and four and twenty elders fell down before the Lamb,</u> having every one of them harps, and golden vials full of odours, which are the prayers of saints.

9 And <u>they sung a new song, saying, Thou art worthy to take the book, and to open the seals thereof: for thou wast slain, and hast redeemed us to God by thy blood out of every kindred, and tongue, and people, and nation;</u>

10 And <u>hast made us unto our God kings and priests: and we shall reign on the earth.</u>

There will be great rejoicing in Heaven when the Lamb takes possession of the book. The four beasts will fall down before the Lamb and the four and twenty elders, with harps of gold and the prayers of saints, will fall down before Him and worship.

Some have supposed that the prayers of saints, mentioned in verse 8, refers to the prayers of saints in Heaven, but there is nothing in the text to suggest that. J. A. Seiss, in his lectures on Revelation, wrote:

Christ has just now been acknowledged as the possessor of the ability and the right to enter with His redeemed ones upon their inheritance. It is time for all the unanswered prayers of all the saints of all the ages to come into remembrance. They will now be answered. The prayer, *Thy kingdom come. Thy will be done on earth, as it is in heaven,* as Christians have ever prayed, will now be answered.

God treasures the prayers of His people. The Psalmist writes that our prayers are as incense coming up before our God.

Let my prayer be set forth before thee as incense; and the lifting up of my hands as the evening sacrifice (Psa. 141:2).

Verse 9 tells us that they, the raptured church, will sing a new song. The new song will be a song of victory and praise. The song says, *Thou art worthy to take the book, and to open the seals thereof: for thou wast slain, and hast redeemed us to God by thy blood out of every kindred, and tongue, and people, and nation.* In verse 10 we read, *And hast made us unto our God kings and priests: and we shall reign on the earth.* That is clear evidence that the breaking of the seals will redeem the earth.

In God's sight we are already kings and

priests, though we are not yet reigning. After Jesus redeems the earth and returns to take possession and sets up His kingdom we will reign with Him.

The Angels Rejoice

11 And I beheld, and <u>I heard the voice of many angels round about the throne</u> and the beasts and the elders: and the number of them was <u>ten thousand times ten thousand, and thousands of thousands;</u>

12 Saying with a loud voice, <u>Worthy is the Lamb that was slain to receive power, and riches, and wisdom, and strength, and honour, and glory, and blessing.</u>

An innumerable company of angels will join in the rejoicing when the earth is redeemed. Verse 11 tells us that there will be ten thousand times ten thousand, and other thousands of angels who will rejoice that the Lamb is worthy to open the seals of the book. They will proclaim, . . . *Worthy is the Lamb that was slain to receive power, and riches, and wisdom, and strength, and honour, and glory, and blessing.*

The angels will have reason to rejoice. They saw Satan fall from Heaven, and they saw Adam and Eve go into sin. They have witnessed the curse upon the earth, and they have witnessed the suffering, sorrow, and death that sin has brought upon mankind. What a rejoicing multitude the angels will be when the seals are loosed on the book of redemption and Jesus takes possession of the earth.

Universal Recognition of the Redeemer

13 And <u>every creature which is in heaven, and on the earth, and under the earth, and such as are in the sea,</u> and all that are in them, heard I saying, <u>Blessing, and honour, and glory, and power, be unto him that sitteth upon the throne, and unto the Lamb for ever and ever.</u>

14 And the <u>four beasts said, Amen.</u> And <u>the four and twenty elders fell down and worshipped him</u> that liveth for ever and ever.

Heaven, earth, and the realm of the wicked dead will join in recognition of the Redeemer when the earth is redeemed. There will be rejoicing in Heaven that will include the holy angels and the redeemed saints. Under the earth lost souls will recognize that Christ is the redeemer of the ruined earth, and at last every knee will bow before Him.

Wherefore God also hath highly exalted him, and given him a name which is above every name: That at the name of Jesus every knee should bow, of things in heaven, and things in earth, and things under the earth (Phil. 2:9, 10).

Chapter 5 closes with the seraphim saying, *"Amen,"* and with the raptured church falling down before the Lord in worship.

There is truly reason for rejoicing in this chapter, but there will be no cause for rejoicing in the next chapter. It will take us through the tribulation and bring us to the terrible judgments that will come upon the earth when Christ comes to take possession of the earth.

Chapter 6

Introduction to Chapter 6

C hapter 6 is the last chapter of section one. In it we have the breaking of the first six seals on the seven-sealed book. The breaking of the seals will take us through the tribulation from the viewpoint of the church and give us the first account of the Second Coming of Christ.

The breaking of the first four seals will show Antichrist's rise to power and his disastrous reign. The breaking of the fifth seal will give us John's vision of martyred saints in glory. The breaking of the sixth seal will show the coming judgments in the heavens and upon the earth, with men from every station in life fleeing and hiding in the dens and rocks of the mountains from the face of God and the wrath of the Lamb.

Section two begins in chapter 7 with the sealing of the hundred and forty-four thousand of all the tribes of Israel. The seventh seal will not be broken until the beginning of chapter 8, after the hundred and forty-four thousand of the twelve tribes of Israel have been sealed. Israel will be included in the redemption of the earth. That is as it should be, for Jesus will rule over Israel in the redeemed earth during the millennium.

Contents of Chapter 6

The Opening of the First Seal

1 And I saw when the Lamb opened one of the seals, and I heard, as it were the noise of thunder, one of the four beasts saying, Come and see.

2 And I saw, and behold a white horse: and he that sat on him had a bow; and a crown was given unto him: and he went forth conquering, and to conquer.

In verse 1 we read that the Lamb opened one of the seals, and John heard one of the four beasts telling him in a voice like thunder to come and see what was about to happen. The loudness of the voice underscored the importance of the vision he was about to see.

When the first seal was broken, John saw Satan's false Christ riding on a white horse. He was imitating the true Christ who will ride on a white horse in His glorious Second Coming as described in Revelation 19:11. When Satan rebelled against God, he boasted that he would be like God (Isa. 14:14). Still attempting to be like God, at the beginning of the tribulation he will send Antichrist, his imitation of the true Christ, into the world.

When Antichrist appears on the white horse he will have a bow and a crown. The bow is a primitive weapon, but it indicates that he had been a soldier or a general in some army before his crown was given to him. Antichrist will not have great strength in the beginning. Daniel prophesied that he will work deceitfully and will become strong with a small people.

And after the league made with him he shall work deceitfully: for he shall come up, and shall become strong with a small people (Dan. 11:23).

After the rapture of the church the world will be in a state of turmoil. So many people will be missing from all nations there will be a great decrease in the sale of all kinds of merchandise. As a result businesses will fail and governments will topple and fall. Democracies will be unable to cope with such chaotic conditions, and in the void new kings will rise and come to power. In time ten kings will take control of the nations of the world.

The Book of Daniel contains prophecies that outline the history of the world from the time of Nebuchadnezzar, king of Babylon, until the Second Coming of Christ. In chapter 2, Daniel interprets Nebuchadnezzar's dream of a great image, with head of gold, breast and arms of silver, belly and thighs of brass, legs of iron, and feet of iron and clay.

In the interpretation Daniel told King Nebuchadnezzar that he was the head of gold, and that the other parts of the image foretold the rise of governments that would follow his reign.

The breast and arms of silver foretold the rise of Media-Persia, the second world empire. The belly and thighs of brass foretold the rise of the third world empire, the Grecian Empire. The legs of iron foretold the rise of the Roman Empire, the fourth world empire. The feet of iron and clay foretold the unstable governments of the last days, and the ten toes foretold the rise of the ten kings that will come to power after the rapture.

Daniel had a vision that gave some added details of what will happen in the last days. He saw a beast with ten horns that represent the same ten kings that were represented by the ten toes of Nebuchadnezzar's image (Dan. 7:7). His vision also predicted the rise of Antichrist. In verse 8 he wrote that a little horn will come up among the ten horns and will pluck up three of the horns by the roots. The little horn will defeat three of the ten kings in war on his way to world domination.

And the ten horns out of this kingdom are ten kings that shall arise: and another shall rise after them; and he shall be diverse from the first, and he shall subdue three kings (Dan. 7:24).

Antichrist will be a master negotiator, and he will persuade the seven remaining kings to turn over their kingdoms to him. In all probability they will be among the puppet kings that will serve under him after he comes to power. Daniel wrote that this king will come in peaceably and obtain the kingdom by flatteries.

And in his estate shall stand up a vile person, to whom they shall not give the honour of the kingdom: but he shall come in peaceably, and obtain the kingdom by flatteries (Dan. 11:21).

The Opening of the Second Seal

3 And when he had opened the second seal, I heard the second beast say, Come and see.

*4 And <u>there went out another horse
that was red: and power was given to
him that sat thereon to take peace from
the earth,</u> and that they should kill one
another: and <u>there was given unto him
a great sword.</u>*

Antichrist will come to power promising
peace, but he will soon break his promise and
plunge the world into war. With the breaking of
the second seal Antichrist will change from the
white horse of peace to the red horse of war, and
he will be given a great sword. The great sword
may represent a super weapon of the future that
will make Antichrist invincible. In Revelation
13:4 we have men saying, . . . *who is able to
make war with him?*

The Opening of the Third Seal

*5 And <u>when he had opened the third
seal</u>, I heard the third beast say, Come
and see. And I beheld, and <u>lo a black
horse; and he that sat on him had a pair
of balances in his hand.</u>*

*6 And I heard a voice in the midst
of the four beasts say, <u>A measure of
wheat for a penny, and three measures
of barley for a penny; and see thou hurt
not the oil and the wine.</u>*

By the time Antichrist changes to the black

horse he will be in position to fix prices and control all commerce. The wars he has fought on his way to world domination will have caused shortages, and the rationing he will impose will be worse than it was during World War II. During that war gasoline, tires, coffee, sugar, and other commodities were rationed. Under Antichrist only oil and wine will be exempt from rationing. In Revelation 13 we are told that no one will be allowed to buy or sell unless they have the mark of the beast in their foreheads or in their hands (Rev. 13:16, 17).

The Opening of the Fourth Seal

7 And <u>when he had opened the fourth seal,</u> I heard the voice of the fourth beast say, Come and see.

8 And <u>I looked, and behold a pale horse:</u> and <u>his name that sat on him was Death, and Hell followed with him.</u> And <u>power was given unto them</u> over the fourth part of the earth, <u>to kill with sword, and with hunger, and with death, and with the beasts of the earth.</u>

With the opening of the fourth seal Antichrist will change to the pale horse. Death and hell will follow him, and his reign will become a reign of terror. During that time men will die in battle, from hunger, and from wild beasts that will leave their normal habitat and devour them. Millions more will die at the hand of Antichrist.

Suffering will be extreme under the reign of Antichrist. People always suffer under the reign of a wicked king. The writer of Proverbs has well said, *As a roaring lion, and a ranging bear; so is a wicked ruler over the poor people (Prov. 28:15).*

The Opening of the Fifth Seal

9 And <u>when he had opened the fifth seal, I saw under the altar the souls of them that were slain for the word of God, and for the testimony which they held:</u>

10 And they cried with a loud voice, saying, How long, O Lord, holy and true, dost thou not judge and avenge our blood on them that dwell on the earth?

11 And white robes were given unto every one of them; and it was said unto them, that they should rest yet for a little season, until their fellowservants also and their brethren, that should be killed as they were, should be fulfilled.

After the opening of the fifth seal in verse 9, John saw the souls of people under the altar who had been slain during the tribulation. This tells us that there will be saved people on earth during the tribulation, and many of them will die for refusing to submit to Antichrist and receive his mark.

The Opening of the Sixth Seal

12 And I beheld when he had opened the sixth seal, and, <u>lo, there was a great earthquake; and the sun became black as sackcloth of hair, and the moon became as blood;</u>

13 <u>And the stars of heaven fell unto the earth,</u> even as a fig tree casteth her untimely figs, when she is shaken of a mighty wind.

14 And <u>the heaven departed as a scroll</u> when it is rolled together; <u>and every mountain and island were moved out of their places.</u>

15 And <u>the kings of the earth, and the great men, and the rich men, and the chief captains, and the mighty men, and every bondman, and every free man, hid themselves in the dens and in the rocks of the mountains;</u>

16 <u>And said to the mountains and rocks, Fall on us, and hide us from the face of him that sitteth on the throne, and from the wrath of the Lamb:</u>

17 <u>For the great day of his wrath is come;</u> and who shall be able to stand?

The opening of the sixth seal brings us to

the Second Coming of Christ. In verse 17 it is called, *the great day of his wrath.*

The preceding verses from The Revelation tell us that at the time of the Second Coming mountains and islands will be moved out of their places by a great earthquake. The sun and the moon will stop giving light. The heavens will be rolled up like a scroll, and stars will fall from Heaven.

Meteors are often called falling stars. They are not uncommon, and on occasions many of them are visible. There was a night in 1883 when meteors fell like snowflakes. It was estimated that many thousands of the so-called shooting stars fell every hour throughout the night. Many thought that the end of the world had come. That display of falling meteors does not compare to the falling stars of the end time.

Men Will Hide for Fear

The upheavals in the heavens and on the earth will be so terrible that people will flee to the rocks and mountains and hide.

In this way many will survive the terrible judgments that will accompany the Second Coming. According to the Gospel of Matthew enough will survive to continue as nations after the coming of Christ. In Matthew they are called sheep nations and goat nations. Jesus will judge the sheep and goat nations after His Second Coming (Matt. 25:31-46).

Isaiah wrote of dreadful judgments that will come upon the earth and the heavens at the time of the Second Coming. He called it the day of the Lord and said that He would come with wrath and fierce anger.

> *Behold, the day of the LORD cometh, cruel both with wrath and fierce anger, to lay the land desolate: and he shall destroy the sinners thereof out of it (Isa. 13:9).*

Further, he wrote that the earth will be moved out of its place. Such a movement of the earth will make the stars appear to fall, or it may be that the stars will also be moved from their places. Isaiah also predicted great signs in the heavens on the day of the Lord. A part of his prophecy follows.

> *For the stars of heaven and the constellations thereof shall not give their light: the sun shall be darkened in his going forth, and the moon shall not cause her light to shine.*
>
> *Therefore I will shake the heavens, and the earth shall remove out of her place, in the wrath of the LORD of hosts, and in the day of his fierce anger (Isa. 13:10, 13).*

Isaiah also predicted:

> *The earth shall reel to and fro like*

> *a drunkard, and shall be removed like a*
> *cottage; and the transgression thereof*
> *shall be heavy upon it; and it shall fall,*
> *and not rise again (Isa. 24:20).*

The breaking of the sixth seal will bring us to the judgments of the Second Coming of Christ. In verses 16 and 17 of this chapter of The Revelation men recognize that the great day of the wrath of the Lamb has come.

This chapter of The Revelation brings us to the end of section one. In it we have seen the Second Coming from the viewpoint of the church. In section two we will go through the tribulation from the viewpoint of Israel and come to the Second Coming for the second time. In section three we will go through the tribulation from the viewpoint of the Gentile nations and come to the Second Coming for the third time.

Chapter 7

Section 2 Chapters 7-11

Introduction to Chapter 7

*T*he phrase, *after these things,* in the opening verse of this chapter tells us that section one is finished. We now begin the study of section two. Many believe that chapter 7 should be considered a parenthesis, but the structure of The Revelation does not support that position.

As stated earlier, chapters 7 through 11 will take us through the tribulation and bring us to the Second Coming of Christ for the second time. Section one covered these events from the viewpoint of the church. Section two covers them from the viewpoint of Israel. Section three will take us through the tribulation and to the Second Coming from the viewpoint of the Gentile nations.

Verses 1 through 3 of this chapter sets the stage for the sealing of a hundred and forty-four thousand men from the twelve tribes of Israel. Verses 4 through 8 covers their sealing, and verses 9 through 17 gives a view of tribulation converts rejoicing in Heaven.

Contents of Chapter 7

1. Restraining the winds (verses 1-3)
2. The hundred and forty-four thousand (verse 4)
3. The names of the twelve tribes (verses 5-8)
4. The saved multitude (verses 9, 10)
5. Rejoicing around the throne (verses 11, 12)
6. The elder's question (verse 13)
7. The answer to the elder's question (verse 14)
8. The blessed Redeemed (verses 15, 16)
9. The Lord's tender care (verse 17)

Restraining the Winds

1 And after these things I saw four angels standing on the four corners of the earth, holding the four winds of the earth, that the wind should not blow on the earth, nor on the sea, nor on any tree.

2 And I saw another angel ascending from the east, having the seal of the living God: and he cried with a loud voice to the four angels, to whom it was given to hurt the earth and the sea,

3 Saying, Hurt not the earth, neither the sea, nor the trees, till we have sealed the servants of our God in their foreheads.

Verse 1 tells us that four angels are to restrain the four winds so they will not blow on the earth, nor the sea, or on any tree until the hundred and forty-four thousand are sealed in their foreheads.

Four is the number of the earth. There are four points of the compass. There are four seasons in the year. There are four phases of the moon. There are four tides in a day, two high tides and two low tides, and there are four watches in the night, and, as covered in the last chapter, there will be four world governments before the Second Coming of Christ.

Verse 2 tells of an angel from the east with the seal of God. This angel cried in a loud voice to the four angels of the winds that they should not hurt the earth or the sea until the servants of God were sealed in their foreheads. It is noteworthy that the hundred and forty-four thousand are servants of God before they are sealed, and they will continue to serve God after they are sealed.

In section one the tribulation will not begin until after the church is translated to Heaven. In section two the tribulation will not begin until the hundred and forty-four thousand are sealed.

Israel is not mentioned in section one. That is because Israel is set aside during the church age. The church is not mentioned in section two, because it is no longer on the earth, and God has turned again to Israel.

During the church age temporary blindness

has happened in part to Israel, and God is saving people from among the Gentiles. The blindness of Israel will continue until the church is raptured. After that God will turn again to Israel. Paul made this clear in his letter to the Romans.

> *For I would not, brethren, that ye should be ignorant of this mystery, lest ye should be wise in your own conceits; that <u>blindness in part is happened to Israel, until the fullness of the Gentiles be come in</u> (Rom. 11:25).*

God's future plans for Israel was covered in more detail during the church council that was held in Jerusalem in A.D. 46. The council was convened to determine whether or not Gentile Christians should be circumcised. During the council, James, the half brother of Jesus, and the leader of the Jerusalem church, spoke about God's present and future plans for Israel. He said that in the present dispensation God is saving Gentiles, but He is not finished with Israel. He is going to turn again to Israel and use them to reach more Gentiles. His prediction, given below, will be fulfilled during the tribulation.

> *Simeon hath declared how God at the first did visit the Gentiles, to take out of them a people for his name. And to this agree the words of the prophets; as it is written, After this I will return,*

and will build again the tabernacle of David, which is fallen down; and I will build again the ruins thereof, and I will set it up: That the residue of men might seek after the Lord, and all the Gentiles, upon whom my name is called, saith the Lord, who doeth all these things (Acts 15:14-17).

Even in the time when Israel is temporally set aside, God is working out His plan for their future. The forming of the Jewish state, May 14, 1948, was a miraculous fulfillment of prophecy. The prophecy of Isaiah was fulfilled when a nation was born in a day.

Who hath heard such a thing? who hath seen such things? Shall the earth be made to bring forth in one day? or shall a nation be born at once? for as soon as Zion travailed, she bought forth her children (Isa. 66:8).

Many Jews have returned to Israel since their state was formed, but most of them have returned in unbelief. Ezekiel's vision of the valley of dry bones coming together, as recorded in chapter 37, pictures how a dead, scattered nation was to be brought together and come to life. In verse 11 he wrote, . . . *these bones are the whole house of Israel.*

In Ezekiel's vision the scattered bones came

together and flesh and sinew came upon them, but the passage says, . . . *there was no breath in them (Ezek. 37:8).* That pictures the nation of Israel regathered in unbelief, but they will not always remain in unbelief. Paul wrote concerning them:

> *For if thou* (Gentiles) *wert cut out of the olive tree which is wild by nature, and wert grafted contrary to nature into a good olive tree: how much more shall these,* (Israelis) *which be the natural branches, be grafted into their own olive tree? (Rom. 11:24).*

Further Paul wrote in verse 26,

> *And so all Israel shall be saved: as it is written, There shall come out of Sion the Deliverer, and shall turn away ungodliness from Jacob.*

The Hundred and Forty-four Thousand

> *4 And I heard the number of them which were sealed: and there were sealed an hundred and forty and four thousand of all the tribes of the children of Israel.*

Several false religions teach that the hundred and forty-four thousand represent one Gentile group or another, but their claims are unfounded. God's Word clearly says that the hundred and forty-four thousand will be sealed out of the twelve tribes of Israel. Therefore they cannot represent any Gentile group.

Twelve is the number of Israel. Jacob had twelve sons, and there were twelve tribes of Israel. One hundred and forty-four, a multiple of twelve, represents the entire nation of Israel. The city John saw descending from Heaven has twelve foundations and twelve gates of pearl. The names of the twelve apostles are written on the foundations of the city, and the names of the twelve tribes of Israel are written on the twelve gates.

The Names of the Twelve Tribes

5 *Of the tribe of Juda were sealed twelve thousand. Of the tribe of Reuben were sealed twelve thousand. Of the tribe of Gad were sealed twelve thousand.*

6 *Of the tribe of Aser were sealed twelve thousand. Of the tribe of Nepthalim were sealed twelve thousand. Of the tribe of Manasses were sealed twelve thousand.*

7 *Of the tribe of Simeon were sealed twelve thousand. Of the tribe of Levi were sealed twelve thousand. Of the tribe of Issachar were sealed twelve thousand.*

*8 Of the tribe of Zabulon were
sealed twelve thousand. Of the tribe of
Joseph were sealed twelve thousand. Of
the tribe of Benjamin were sealed twelve
thousand.*

An equal number of these servants of God
will be sealed from each of the twelve tribes.
They will be God's evangelists during the tribulation, and the greatest revival of all time will
take place. Verse 9 tells of millions being saved
out of all the nations of the earth.

The Saved Multitude

*9 After this I beheld, and, lo, a great
multitude, which no man could number,
of all nations, and kindreds, and people,
and tongues, stood before the throne,
and before the Lamb, clothed with white
robes, and palms in their hands;*

*10 And cried with a loud voice, say-
ing, Salvation to our God which sitteth
upon the throne, and unto the Lamb.*

Under the reign of Antichrist, most of the
saved, perhaps all of them, will be killed for their
faith and will go immediately into the presence
of the Lord. They will be before the throne of
God and before the Lamb. They will be clothed
with white robes. They will have palms in their
hands, and they will shout praises to God. This

multitude will be so great that they cannot be counted.

Rejoicing Around the Throne

11 And all the angels stood round about the throne, and about the elders and the four beasts, and fell before the throne on their faces, and worshipped God,

12 Saying, Amen: Blessing, and glory, and wisdom, and thanksgiving, and honour, and power, and might, be unto our God for ever and ever. Amen.

The rejoicing over the multitude being saved will be much like the rejoicing that occurred after the rapture of the church (Rev. 4:1-11). The same personages will be present, and they will praise God as they did after the rapture.

The Elder's Question

13 And one of the elders answered, saying unto me, What are these which are arrayed in white robes? and whence came they?

From our previous study we know that the elders symbolize the raptured church. This multitude in white robes had not been raptured with the church, so is not surprising that in verse 13 the elders will ask who they are.

The Answer to the Elder's Question

14 And I said unto him, Sir, thou knowest. And he said to me, <u>These are they which came out of great tribulation, and have washed their robes, and made them white in the blood of the Lamb.</u>

Verse 14 tells us that this saved multitude had come out of great tribulation, and that they had been saved in the same way people were saved before the rapture of the church. They had been washed in the blood of the Lamb.

The Blessed Redeemed

15 Therefore are they before the throne of God, and <u>serve him day and night in his temple:</u> and he that sitteth on the throne shall dwell among them.

16 They shall hunger no more, neither thirst any more; neither shall the sun light on them, nor any heat.

This mighty company of tribulation saints will not be part of the church. They will include Jewish converts and they will serve God in the heavenly temple (verse 15). The heavenly temple will be for these Jewish converts. The church will have no need of the temple in Heaven, for God and Jesus will be their temple (Rev. 21:22).

The Lord's Tender Care

17 <u>For the Lamb</u> which is in the midst of the throne <u>shall feed them, and shall lead them unto living fountains of waters: and God shall wipe away all tears from</u> their eyes.

Jesus will take care of the martyred saints of the tribulation. He will feed them and lead them to fountains of living water. They will have had tears enough on earth because of the persecution of the Antichrist. Now they are beyond suffering and sorrow. God will wipe away all tears from their eyes, and they will never cry again.

Chapter 8

Introduction to Chapter 8

*T*he sealing of the hundred and forty-four thousand men of Israel in chapter 7 comes before the breaking of the seventh seal in this chapter. The breaking of the seventh seal finishes the redemption of the earth and shows that Israel will be included in that redemption. We saw in chapter 4 that the church has been translated to Heaven. In this chapter God has turned again to Israel, and in this section we will see God again dealing with Israel.

Contents of Chapter 8

The Seventh Seal Opened

1 And when he had opened <u>the sev-</u>
<u>*enth seal, there was silence in heaven*</u>
<u>*about the space of half an hour.*</u>

The opening of the seventh seal is not an introduction to the sounding of the seventh trumpets. We are only told that when the seventh seal was opened there was silence in Heaven for half an hour.

Some writers have suggested that the period of silence will be in anticipation of the judgments that are about to come upon the earth, but the text does not say that. Nor does it say what the silence symbolizes. It may be that this will be a silence of rest. God created the earth in six days and rested on the Sabbath. It may be that when Christ redeems the earth it will bring a rest so complete that all Heaven will be silent for half an hour.

Chapter 8 will take us through the sounding of the first four trumpets and the announcement of the three woes that are to come upon the earth. The sounding of the last three trumpets in chapter 9 will bring the three woes.

The Seven Trumpets

2 And <u>I saw the seven angels which</u>
<u>*stood before God; and to them were*</u>
<u>*given seven trumpets.*</u>

John often introduces a subject before he writes about it. In verse 2 he introduces the seven angels with the seven trumpets, but before he writes about them, he writes in verses 3 through 5, about the prayers of the saints and the things that will happen before the sounding of the first trumpet. It is not until verse 6 that he mentions the angels again. Then it is only to tell us that they are preparing themselves to sound their trumpets. It is not until verse 7 that we read of the sounding of the first trumpet.

The Prayers of Saints

3 And <u>another angel came</u> and stood at the altar, having a golden censer; and <u>there was given unto him much incense, that he should offer it with the prayers of all saints upon the golden altar which was before the throne.</u>

4 And the smoke of the incense, which came with the prayers of the saints, ascended up before God out of the angel's hand.

5 And <u>the angel took the censer, and filled it with fire of the altar, and cast it into the earth: and there were voices, and thunderings, and lightnings, and an earthquake.</u>

In verse 3 another angel, not one of the seven angels with the trumpets, is seen standing before the golden altar with a golden censer in his hand. He is given much incense to offer with the prayers of all the saints.

This is not the first mention of the prayers of the saints. In the first section of The Revelation, we read of . . . *golden vials full of odours, which are the prayers of saints (Rev. 5:8).*

It is well to note here that saints does not mean people who have been canonized by the Catholic church. All saved people are saints. Children of God are called saints 61 times in the New Testament.

The angel before the altar offered the prayers of all the saints with much incense. After that he filled the censer with fire from the altar and cast it into the earth. There followed voices, thunderings, lightnings, and an earthquake.

The prayers mentioned in verse 4 are apparently unanswered prayers that are reserved to be answered at the time when Christ will take control of the earth. Through the centuries some prayers have remained unanswered. Now they will be answered.

The Angels Prepare to Sound Their Trumpets

6 And <u>the seven angels</u> which had the seven trumpets <u>prepared themselves to sound.</u>

We have no way of knowing what preparations the angels will make, but we know that terrible judgments will follow the sounding of each of the seven trumpets.

The First Trumpet Sounded

7 The first angel sounded, and there followed hail and fire mingled with blood, and they were cast upon the earth: and the third part of trees was burnt up, and all green grass was burnt up.

The sounding of the first trumpet will cause hail and fire, mingled with blood, to be cast upon the earth. This judgment will burn up a third of the trees and all the grass. Since trees and grass produce oxygen, this will reduce the amount of oxygen for men and animals to breathe. Far worse judgments are soon to come.

The Second Trumpet Sounded

8 And the second angel sounded, and as it were a great mountain burning with fire was cast into the sea: and the third part of the sea became blood;

9 And the third part of the creatures which were in the sea, and had life, died; and the third part of the ships were destroyed.

When the second trumpet is sounded something that looks like a burning mountain will fall into the sea. It will not be a mountain; it will only look like a mountain. Scientists tell us that it is only a matter of time until a large meteor from outer space will strike the earth with devastating results. That is possibly what will happen with the sounding of the second trumpet. Whatever this burning object may be, it will fill a third of the sea with blood, kill a third of all life in the sea, and destroy a third of the ships.

The Third Trumpet Sounded

10 And the third angel sounded, and there fell a great star from heaven, burning as it were a lamp, and it fell upon the third part of the rivers, and upon the fountains of waters;

11 And the name of the star is called Wormwood: and the third part of the waters became wormwood; and many men died of the waters, because they were made bitter.

The sounding of the third trumpet will cause a meteor called wormwood to fall. It will be directed against the rivers and other bodies of water.

Wormwood is a poisonous, bitter plant, and it is symbolic of the bitter calamities that will come upon the earth after the sounding of the third trumpet. Apparently this falling meteor will break up before it lands, for it will land on many bodies of water. It will cause a third of the water on earth to become bitter and poisonous. As a result a third part of the population of the earth will die.

The Fourth Trumpet Sounded

12 And the fourth angel sounded, and the third part of the sun was smitten, and the third part of the moon, and the third part of the stars; so as the third part of them was darkened, and the day shone not for a third part of it, and the night likewise.

The sounding of the fourth trumpet will affect the sun, moon, and stars, and a third part of the days will be dark, and a third part of the nights will be without the light of the moon or a single star. Worse things will come to pass with the sounding of the last three trumpets.

The Three Woes Announced

13 And I beheld, and heard an angel flying through the midst of heaven, saying with a loud voice, Woe, woe, woe, to the inhabiters of the earth by reason of the other voices of the trumpet of the three angels, which are yet to sound!

Four of the seven angels have sounded their trumpets in this chapter. The sounding of the remaining three trumpets, described in chapters 9 through 11, will bring judgments upon the earth so terrible that they are called woes. The first two woes will take us into the nether realm and give us a view of Satan and his evil forces that have never before been seen. The third woe will bring the terrible judgments that will be visited upon the earth at the time of the Second Coming of Christ.

Chapter 9

Introduction to Chapter 9

*C*hapter 9 begins with a star falling from Heaven and continues with the sounding of the three remaining trumpets and the announcement of the three woes.

The remaining chapters of this section will finish the last half of the tribulation, and they will show Satan's involvement in the things that will come to pass before the Second Coming of Christ.

When the fifth angel sounds his trumpet the forces of darkness will become involved in the tribulation. Satan and his fallen angels and his demons will do their worst to the earth, the sea, the heavenly bodies, and to mankind.

Contents of Chapter 9

1. A falling star (verse 1)
2 The opening of the pit (verse 2)
3. Locusts from the pit (verse 3)
4. The power of the locusts limited (verse 4)
5. Five months of torment (verses 5, 6)

6. The description of the locusts (verses 7-10)
7. The king of the locusts (verse 11)
8. Two woes to come (verse 12)
9. The sixth trumpet sounded (verses 13-15)
10. The description of the army (verses 16, 17)
11. The terrible toll (verses 18, 19)
12. Punishment does not cause repentance (verses 20, 21)

A Falling Star

1 And <u>the fifth angel sounded, and I saw a star fall from heaven unto the earth: and to him was given the key of the bottomless pit</u> (abussos = Abyss).

When the fifth angel sounded his trumpet John saw a star fall from Heaven. The star was an angel, but he was not a good angel. Only evil angels fall from Heaven. Further, this falling angel is not called powerful or glorious as were other angels. This is clearly one of Satan's angels.

This angel did not have the key to the abyss until it was given to him. We are not told why God will permit the key to the abyss to be given to a fallen angel. Perhaps that will be God's way to punish wicked men. Or it may be God's way to show how dreadful conditions are in the abyss. Whatever the reason, the opening of the abyss will bring dire consequences to people on earth.

This angel may well be Apollyon, the angel of the bottomless pit. He may also be the king of the demons that are confined in the pit. (See verse 11 of this chapter.)

The Opening of the Pit

2 And he opened the bottomless pit; and there arose a smoke out of the pit, as the smoke of a great furnace; and the sun and the air were darkened by reason of the smoke of the pit.

When the pit is opened smoke will billow from it and darken the air. Ashes from a volcano often darken the sun for days, but the smoke from the abyss will be darker than the smoke from any volcano, and it will bring punishment to wicked men such as the world has never known.

Locusts from the Pit

3 And there came out of the smoke locusts upon the earth: and unto them was given power, as the scorpions of the earth have power.

Some writers believe that the locusts from the pit will be demon spirits, but they will most likely be demon-possessed creatures of some unknown variety. One reason for believing this is that demons are invisible. These creatures will be visible. Further, demons do not attack men with stings. They possess men and torment them from within.

The Power of the Locusts Limited

4 And it was commanded them that they should not hurt the grass of the earth, neither any green thing, neither any tree; but only those men which have not the seal of God in their foreheads.

The locusts that come from the pit will not be allowed to damage vegetation as locusts normally do. Also, they will not be allowed to attack the men of Israel who have the seal of God in their foreheads. These sealed men of Israel will be protected while they do the work God has for them to do, but wicked men will not be protected from the locusts.

Five Months of Torment

5 And to them it was given that they should not kill them, but that they should be tormented five months: and their torment was as the torment of a scorpion, when he striketh a man.

6 And in those days shall men seek death, and shall not find it; and shall desire to die, and death shall flee from them.

The strike of a scorpion is painful and sometimes fatal. The strike of the locusts from the abyss will be painful, but it will not be fatal. Their strike will make men suffer so much they will want to die, but they will be denied the relief of death. The text says that death will flee from them.

The Description of the Locusts

7 And the shapes of the locusts were like unto horses prepared unto battle; and on their heads were as it were crowns like gold, and their faces were as the faces of men.

8 And they had hair as the hair of women, and their teeth were as the teeth of lions.

9 And they had breastplates, as it were breastplates of iron; and the sound of their wings was as the sound of chariots of many horses running to battle.

10 And they had tails like unto scorpions, and there were stings in their tails: and their power was to hurt men five months.

The locusts will be awesome creatures. They will look like horses prepared for battle. Their heads will look like they are crowned with gold. Their faces will look like the faces of men. Their hair will look like women's hair, and their teeth will look like lions' teeth. Even their appearance will fill men's hearts with fear.

The King of the Locusts

11 <u>And they had a king over them,</u>
<u>which is the angel of the bottomless pit,</u>
whose name in the Hebrew tongue is
Abaddon, but in the Greek tongue hath
his name Apollyon.

The locusts will have a king over them. His
name is Abaddon in Hebrew and Apollyon in
Greek. His name being given both in Hebrew
and in Greek suggest that he is the enemy of both
Jews and Gentiles.

This chapter gives us a glimpse of the orga-
nized kingdom of Satan. In Ephesians 6:12 Paul
describes his kingdom as follows.

For we wrestle not against flesh and
blood, but against principalities, against
powers, against the rulers of the dark-
ness of this world, against spiritual
wickedness in high places.

Paul wrote of principalities and of the rulers
of the darkness of this world. A principality is a
government ruled over by a prince. This may
include the king of the abyss. No doubt there are
other principalities. The king of the abyss will
control the locusts. In the next verse we are told
that the coming of the locusts is the first woe.
No other word can adequately describe the ter-

rible suffering that the locusts will cause.

Two Woes to Come

12 One woe is past; and, behold, there come two woes more hereafter.

The first woe will be so terrible it will cause men to desire death. There are two woes yet to come, each of them more terrible than the last.

The Sixth Trumpet Sounded

13 And the sixth angel sounded, and I heard a voice from the four horns of the golden altar which is before God,

14 Saying to the sixth angel which had the trumpet, Loose the four angels which are bound in the great river Euphrates.

15 And the four angels were loosed, which were prepared for an hour, and a day, and a month, and a year, for to slay the third part of men.

When sixth trumpet is sounded a voice will come from the golden altar which is before God. The earthly altar of incense stood before the holy place in the temple. This golden altar before God will be in the most holy place of all.

We are not told who was speaking from the golden altar, but we are told that the message was directed to the angel who was to sound the sixth trumpet. He was told to loose the four angels that were bound in the Euphrates River.

The four angels which were bound in the Euphrates River are fallen angels. Good angels are never bound. Jude wrote about angels that were bound in chains of darkness for leaving their appointed place and committing sexual sins (Jude 6, 7). This is an evidence that fallen angels are bound for specific sins.

We are not told why God will allow fallen angels to be in Satan's army. We are only told that it will happen. These angels will be prepared and loosed at a predetermined day and hour. They will slay a third of the men on earth. From verse 16 we learn that they will command an army of two hundred thousand thousand. That will be an army of two hundred million.

The Description of the Army

16 And the number of the army of the horsemen were two hundred thousand thousand: and I heard the number of them.

17 And thus <u>I saw the horses</u> in the vision, <u>and them that sat on them,</u> <u>having breastplates of fire, and of jacinth, and brimstone: and the heads of the horses were as the heads of lions; and out of their mouths issued fire and smoke</u>

and brimstone.

An army of two hundred million wicked spirit-beings will attack people on earth after the angels bound in the Euphrates River are loosed.

The forces John saw do not compare to anything on earth. God's heavenly army is described as horses and chariots of fire (2 Kings 6:17). God's army defies description. The spiritual army of Satan also defies description. John described what he saw as horses with heads that looked like lions with fire and smoke and brimstone coming from their mouths. The riders on the horses were wearing breastplates of fire, and jacinth, and brimstone. Fire is fiery red. Jacinth is a purple red, and brimstone is a sulphur-yellow. No army of mortal men can fit that description.

The Terrible Toll

18 By these three was the third part *of men killed,* by the fire, and by the *smoke, and by the brimstone, which issued out of their mouths.*

19 For their power is in their mouth, and in their tails: for their tails were like unto serpents, and had heads, and with them they do hurt.

This will be the most deadly war of all time, and it will appear that Satan has won the war. His demons and fallen angels may dance with glee, thinking that they have won, but this is not the end. The Battle of Armageddon is yet to come. In that battle all of Antichrist's armies of mortal men and all of Satan's forces of evil beings will be defeated.

Punishment Will Not Cause Repentance

20 And the rest of the men which were not killed by these plagues yet <u>repented not of the works of their hands, that they should not worship devils, and idols of gold, and silver, and brass, and stone, and of wood: which neither can see, nor hear, nor walk:</u>

21 <u>Neither repented they of their murders, nor of their sorceries, nor of their fornication, nor of their thefts.</u>

Wicked men who are not killed in the war will not repent. They will continue to worship idols that represent the demons they are serving.

Punishment alone does not cause men to turn to God. If punishment would cause men to repent, all the prisoners in the jails and penitentiaries of the world would repent.

Chapter 10

Introduction to Chapter 10

*I*n this chapter John saw a mighty angel come down from Heaven and stand upon the land and the sea, and he heard the angel proclaim in a voice like the roar of a lion that time should be no longer. Following that, seven thunders utter their voices, but John is forbidden to write what the seven thunders said.

The mystery of God is finished. John is commanded to eat the little book that the angel had in his hand, and he is told that he must prophecy again before many peoples, and nations, and tongues, and kings.

This chapter sets the stage for the second and third woes. In verse 13 of chapter 11 we have the second woe, and in verse 14 we are told that the third woe will come quickly. The third woe will follow the sounding of the seventh trumpet in Revelation 11:15, but not until Revelation 12:12 are we told the cause of the third woe.

Contents of Chapter 10

1. The mighty angel (verse 1)
2. The little book (verse 2)
3. The seven thunders (verses 3, 4)
4. Christ's proclamation (verses 5, 6)
5. The mystery of God (verse 7)
6. John commanded to eat the little book (verses 8,9)
7. The taste of the book John ate (verses 10, 11).

The Mighty Angel

1 And I saw another mighty angel come down from heaven, <u>clothed with a cloud: and a rainbow was upon his head, and his face was as it were the sun, and his feet as pillars of fire:</u>

The mighty angel that John saw come down from Heaven can only be the Lord Jesus Christ. Nowhere in the Bible is there a description of an angel, clothed with a cloud, wearing a rainbow upon his head, with a face like the sun, and feet like pillars of fire.

This description is much like the first vision John had of the glorified Lord in chapter 1. Further, in chapter 11, verse 3, the angel calls the two heavenly witnesses, *My witnesses.* A mere angel would not have done that.

It is not unheard of for Christ to appear as an angel. In the Old Testament the Son of God was called the Angel of the Lord. In Exodus 3:2 we have the Angel of the Lord appearing to Moses as a flame of fire in a bush. In verse 4 we read that the Lord saw Moses turn aside to see the bush. In verse 7 the Lord spoke to Moses, and in verse 14 God said to Moses, *I AM THAT I AM.*

As already stated, in this section God is dealing with Israel, so it is not surprising that Christ should come on the scene as the Angel of the Lord.

The Little Book

2 And he had in his hand a little book open: and <u>he set his right foot upon the sea, and his left foot on the earth,</u>

In verse 2 we see Christ standing on the sea and on the earth with an open book in His hand. That is a fitting symbol of Jesus taking possession of the world that Satan has controlled since the fall of Adam and Eve.

Christ, as the mighty angel with the little book open in His hand, makes the astounding proclamation that time should be no longer (verse 6). That indicates that the little book is the book of proclamation.

The Seven Thunders

3 And cried with <u>a loud voice, as when a lion roareth:</u> and when he had cried, <u>seven thunders uttered their voices.</u>

4 And when the seven thunders had uttered their voices, I was about to write: and I heard a voice from heaven saying unto me, Seal up those things which the seven thunders uttered, and write them not.

In verse 4 John heard seven thunders speak. He understood what the thunders said, but he was forbidden to write what they said. We only know that thunder is loud and that it is frightening. Thunder is caused by lightning, and lightning precedes a storm. The loud voices of these seven thunders may have indicated that the storm of God's most severe judgments were drawing near.

Christ's Proclamation

5 And the angel which I saw stand upon the sea and upon the earth lifted up his hand to heaven,

6 And sware by him that liveth for ever and ever, who created heaven, and the things that therein are, and the earth, and the things that therein are, and the sea, and the things which are therein, that there should be time no longer:

In verse 6 the Angel of the Lord proclaims that there should be time no longer. This does not mean that time had ended and eternity had begun. It simply means that there would be delay no longer.

The Mystery of God

*7 But <u>in the days of the voice of the
seventh angel</u>, when he shall begin to
sound, <u>the mystery of God should be finished, as he hath declared to his servants
the prophets.</u>*

Verse 7 tells us that the mystery of God will
be finished after the sounding of the seventh
trumpet. The sounding of the seventh trumpet
will bring us again to the Second Coming of
Christ, and the mystery of God will be solved.

There are five mysteries in The Revelation.
There is the mystery of the seven stars, and the
mystery of the seven golden candlesticks in chapter 1, verse 20. There is the mystery of what the
seven thunders said in verses 2 and 3 of this chapter, and the mystery of God in verse 7. The fifth
mystery is the mystery of the name of the great
harlot, in Revelation 17:5.

The mystery of the seven stars, the seven
candlesticks, and the name of the harlot are explained in the text, but the mystery of what the
thunders said is not given. The mystery of God
is not explained here, but it is explained elsewhere in the Bible.

Men have made many attempts to explain
the meaning of the mystery of God, but they had

only to look in the book of Romans to find the meaning. Paul was quite explicit about its meaning.

> *For I would not, brethren, that ye should be ignorant of this mystery, lest ye should be wise in your own conceits; that blindness in part is happened to Israel, until the fulness of the Gentiles be come in (Rom. 11:25).*

The church age was a mystery to the Old Testament prophets. They did not understand that God would set Israel aside while He worked through the church. Nor did they understand that God would turn again to Israel after the church had been raptured out of the world. Some scholars have understood this and have written about it. For example, Dr. Revere Franklin Weidner (1851-1915) in his book, *Biblical Theology of the New Testament,* wrote:

> "As stated in chapter 7, we started through the tribulation the second time from the viewpoint of Israel. After Israel goes through the tribulation Christ will return as the heir to the throne of David. The people of Israel will be converted and Christ will reign over them forever. Thus the mystery of God will then be fulfilled."

John Commanded to Eat the Little Book

8 And the voice which I heard from heaven spake unto me again, and said, <u>Go and take the little book which is open in the hand of the angel which standeth upon the sea and upon the earth.</u>

9 And I went unto the angel, and said unto him, Give me the little book. <u>And he said unto me, Take it, and eat it up;</u> and it shall make thy belly bitter, but it shall be in thy mouth sweet as honey.

The little book is no longer needed, so John was commanded to eat it. This is not the first time that Scripture has told of the eating of a book. The prophet, Ezekiel, was commanded to eat a book and then to go and speak to the house of Israel. The book he ate was a book of prophecy.

Moreover, he said unto me, Son of man, eat that thou findest: eat this roll (book) and go speak unto the house of Israel (Ezek. 3:1).

The roll that Ezekiel ate was like the little book that John was commanded to eat. It had a taste like honey (Ezek. 3:3), but delivering its message was bitter. The last verse of Ezekiel, chapter 2 says,

. . . there was written therein, lam-

entations, and mourning, and woe.

The Taste of the Book John Ate

10 And <u>I took the little book</u> out of the angel's hand, <u>and ate it up</u>; and <u>it was in my mouth sweet as honey: and as soon as I had eaten it, my belly was bitter.</u>

11 And he said unto me, <u>Thou must prophesy again</u> <u>before many peoples, and nations, and tongues, and kings.</u>

The little book was sweet to John's taste, but it was bitter to digest. John was told that he would have to prophesy again before peoples, and nations, and tongues, and kings, and that was a bitter message to him.

Chapter 11

Introduction to Chapter 11

*T*his is the final chapter that covers the tribulation from the viewpoint of Israel. It will take us through several events that will transpire during the last half of the tribulation, and it will bring us once again to the Second Coming of Christ.

The chapter clearly states in verse 15 that, *The kingdoms of this world are become the kingdoms of our Lord, and of his Christ; and he shall reign for ever and ever.* Jesus will not begin to reign until after His Second Coming. That makes it clear that this chapter brings us through the tribulation and to the Second Coming for the second time.

The Outline of Chapter 11

1. Measuring the temple (verse 1)
2. The last half of the tribulation (verse 2)
3. The two witnesses (verse 3)
4. The olive trees and candlesticks (verse 4)

5. The power of the witnesses (verses 5, 6)
6. The witness killed (verse 7)
7. The witnesses' bodies left unburied (verse 8)
8. All nations will see their dead bodies (verses 9, 10)
9. The witnesses rise from the dead (verse 11)
10. The witnesses ascend to Heaven (verse 12)
11. The second woe (verse 13)
12. The third woe announced (verse 14)
13. The seventh trumpet sounded (verse 15)
14. The elders rejoice (verses 16, 17)
15. Coming events (verse 18)
16. The heavenly temple opened (verse 19)

Measuring the Earthly Temple

1 And there was given me a reed like unto a rod: and the angel stood, saying, <u>Rise, and measure the temple of God,</u> and the altar, and them that worship therein.

The temple of God in this verse is clearly the earthly temple, as distinguished from the heavenly temple (Rev. 11:19). The earthly temple will be built after the rapture, either before or during the first half of the tribulation. That will have to be, for halfway through the tribulation Antichrist will move into the temple and demand to be worshiped as God (2 Thess. 2:4).

It will be the Jews, not the church, that will worship in the temple. This is another evidence that beginning in chapter 7 we are taken through the tribulation from the Jewish point of view.

The Last Half of the Tribulation

2 But the court which is without the temple leave out, and measure it not; for it is given unto the Gentiles: and <u>the holy city shall they tread under foot forty and two months.</u>

In verse 1 John was told to measure the temple, and in verse 2 he was told not to measure the court. The court will be reserved for the Gentiles, for they will continue to occupy Jerusalem through the remainder of the tribulation.

The Two Witnesses

3 And <u>I will give power unto my two witnesses, and they shall prophesy a thousand two hundred and threescore days, clothed in sackcloth.</u>

At the beginning of the second half of the tribulation God's two witnesses will appear on the earth. God will give them power to perform miracles, and they will prophecy for a thousand two hundred and sixty days. That is the number of days in one half of the tribulation.

The identity of the two witnesses has long been the subject of conjecture. Some think they will be Moses and Elijah. Others think they will be Enoch and Elijah.

The reasoning of those who hold the latter

view is that they believe men can only die once, and since Enoch and Elijah were both taken to Heaven without dying they will come back to earth as the witnesses and die.

It is not true, however, that no one will ever die a second time. For example, Jesus raised Lazarus from the dead, and he had to die again. He also raised the widow's son from the dead, and he had to die again.

In the Bible there are several things that suggest that Moses and Elijah will most likely be the two witnesses. Some of those things are listed below.

1. Moses and Elijah were the last two men mentioned in the Old Testament (Mal. 4:4, 5).

2. Moses and Elijah appeared with Jesus on the Mount of Transfiguration (Matt. 17:3).

3. Moses and Elijah performed the same miracles that the two witnesses will perform.

4. Both Moses and Elijah had men who followed them, Joshua followed Moses, and Elisha followed Elijah.

The Olive Trees and Candlesticks

4 These are the two olive trees, and the two candlesticks standing before the God of the earth.

Verse 4 does not mention the two olive trees and the two candlesticks for the first time. Zechariah had a vision of two golden candlesticks and two olive trees, and wrote that these are the two anointed ones that stand by the Lord of the whole earth.

> *Then answered I, and said unto him, What are these two olive trees upon the right side of the candlestick and upon the left side thereof? Then said he, These are the two anointed ones, that stand by the Lord of the whole earth (Zech. 4: 11, 14).*

The two olive trees are types of Israel. In Romans 11:24 Paul refers to Israel as the good olive tree. That means that the two witnesses will be Jews. Two in the Bible is the number of adequate witness. For that reason there will be two witnesses.

The Power of the Witnesses

> *5 And if any man will hurt them, fire proceedeth out of their mouth, and devoureth their enemies: and if any man will hurt them, he must in this manner be killed.*
>
> *6 These have power to shut heaven, that it rain not in the days of their prophecy: and have power over waters to turn*

them to blood, and to smite the earth
with all plagues, *as often as they will.*

The witnesses will have power to destroy
their enemies with fire, verse 5. They will have
power to cause it not to rain for three and a half
years. They will have power to turn water to
blood and to smite the earth with plagues as often as they will, verse 6.

The Witnesses Killed

7 And when they shall have finished
their testimony, *the beast that ascendeth*
out of the bottomless pit shall make war
against them, and shall overcome them,
and kill them.

God will protect the two witnesses, and they
will be invincible until their ministry is finished.
Even then, only Antichrist, the beast from the
bottomless pit, will be able to kill them.

The Witnesses' Bodies Left Unburied

8 And *their dead bodies shall lie in*
the street of the great city, *which spiri-*
tually is called *Sodom and Egypt, where*
also our Lord was crucified.

The enemies of God's witnesses will be so
glad they are dead, they will leave their bodies
exposed in the streets of the city for all the world
to see.

In verse 8 the city where the witnesses will

be killed is called Sodom and Egypt, then identified as Jerusalem where Jesus was crucified.
Sodom speaks of immorality, and Egypt of idolatry. That tells us that Jerusalem will be a corrupt
and wicked city at the time of the end.

All Nations Will See Their Dead Bodies

*9 And they of the people and
kindreds and tongues and nations shall
see their dead bodies three days and an
half, and shall not suffer their dead bodies to be put in graves.*

*10 And <u>they that dwell upon the
earth shall rejoice over them, and make
merry, and shall send gifts one to another; because these two prophets tormented them</u> that dwelt on the earth.*

When the prophecy was written that all nations would see the dead bodies of the witnesses
in the street of Jerusalem, it would not have been
possible for it to be fulfilled. But it is now possible. Satellite television now makes it possible
for all nations to see things as they are happening anywhere in the world. This is an awesome
Bible prophecy.

The Witnesses Rise From the Dead

*11 And after three days and an half
the spirit of <u>life from God entered into</u>*

them, and they stood upon their feet; and great fear fell upon them which saw them.

After the witnesses have been dead for three and a half days, just as God breathed the breath of life into Adam when He created him, the spirit of life from God will raise them from the dead.

It will cause great consternation through-out the world when people see the witnesses rise from the dead. Doubtless Antichrist will want to kill them again, but God will intervene.

The Witnesses Ascend to Heaven

12 And they heard a great voice from heaven saying unto them, Come up hither. And they ascended up to heaven in a cloud; and their enemies beheld them.

A great voice will invite the resurrected wit-nesses to come up to Heaven, and they will as-cend in a cloud. The figure of a cloud is often used in the Bible.

1. A cloud led Israel during their forty years in the wilderness (Ex. 13:21).

2. A cloud came down on the tabernacle in the wilderness (Ex. 40:34).

3. The temple was filled with a cloud when it was being dedicated (2 Chr. 5:13).

4. Ezekiel saw a cloud and fire and brightness when he was visited by angels (Ezek. 1:4).

5. God spoke from a cloud on the Mount of Transfiguration (Matt. 17:5).

6. Daniel saw Jesus come with the clouds of Heaven (Dan. 7:13).

7. Jesus ascended into Heaven in a cloud (Acts 1:9).

8. We will be caught up in the clouds to meet Jesus at the rapture (1 Thess. 4:17).

9. Jesus will come in the clouds at His glorious appearing (Matt. 24:30).

10. In Psalm 104:3 we read that God makes the clouds His chariot.

> . . . *who maketh the clouds his chariot: who walketh upon the wings of the wind.*

It appears from these and many others passages in the Bible that cloud-like vehicles are used for travel in the spirit world.

The Second Woe

> *13 And the same hour was there a great earthquake, and the tenth part of the city fell, and in the earthquake were slain of men seven thousand: and the remnant were affrighted, and gave glory*

to the God of heaven.

Verse 13 tells of a great earthquake that will destroy a tenth of the city and kill seven thousand men. The next verse says the second woe has passed. That means that this earthquake will be the second woe.

Earthquakes are mentioned five times in The Revelation. The first mention of an earthquake is in chapter 6, verse 12. That earthquake occurred when the sixth seal was broken. That was just before the Second Coming of Christ in section one.

The second earthquake occurred in section two, before the sounding of the first trumpet (Rev. 8:5).

The third earthquake is also in section two. It will occur just before the seventh angel sounds his trumpet (Rev. 11:13). This is the second reference to an earthquake that will come just before the Second Coming of Christ. The first earthquake was in section one.

The fifth mention of an earthquake is in Revelation 16:18. It will be the greatest earthquake in the history of the world, and it will occur at the time of the fall of the city of Babylon.

The Third Woe Announced

14 The second woe is past; and, <u>behold, the third woe cometh quickly.</u>

Verse 14 tells us that the third woe will come quickly after the second woe has passed. The details of the coming of the third woe are not given until chapter 12.

The Seventh Trumpet Sounded

15 And the seventh angel sounded; and there were great voices in heaven, saying, The kingdoms of this world are become the kingdoms of our Lord, and of his Christ; and he shall reign for ever and ever.

The sounding of the seventh trumpet brings the announcement that, *The kingdoms of this world are become the kingdoms of our Lord, and of his Christ; and he shall reign for ever and ever.* That is clearly the announcement of the Second Coming of Christ and the beginning of His eternal kingdom.

The Elders Rejoice

16 And the four and twenty elders, which sat before God on their seats, fell upon their faces, and worshipped God,

17 Saying, We give thee thanks, O Lord God Almighty, which art, and wast, and art to come; because thou hast taken to thee thy great power, and hast reigned.

Verses 16 and 17 give us a view of the twenty-four elders in Heaven falling upon their faces, worshiping God, and thanking Him for taking over the kingdoms of the world. They end by saying that He has already reigned. This makes it clear again that the Second Coming has already occurred. There will be no reign of God over the earth before the Second Coming of Christ.

Coming Events

18 And the <u>nations were angry, and thy wrath is come, and the time of the dead, that they should be judged,</u> and that <u>thou shouldest give reward unto thy servants the prophets, and to the saints,</u> and them that fear thy name, small and great; and shouldest destroy them which destroy the earth.

Verse 18 gives us a list of things that will happen after the Second Coming of Christ.

1. The nations will be angry.

2. This is the time of God's wrath.

3. The wicked dead will be raised.

4. The wicked dead will be judged.

5. The prophets and saints will be rewarded.

6. The wicked will be destroyed.

The Heavenly Temple Opened

19 <u>And the temple of God was</u>

*opened in heaven, and there was seen
in his temple the ark of his testament:
and there were lightnings, and voices,
and thunderings, and an earthquake,
and great hail.*

Verse 19 tells us that the temple will be opened in Heaven. Just as the earthly temple was for the Jews, the heavenly temple will be for the Jews. The church has no need of a temple on earth, and it will have no need of a temple in Heaven. The saved of the church will live in the New Jerusalem, and there will be no temple there. God and the Lamb will be the temple for the redeemed in Heaven (Rev. 21:22).

The opening of the temple in Heaven is a final evidence that section two has taken us through the tribulation and brought us to the Second Coming from the Jewish point of view.

Chapter 12

Introduction to Section Three

We come now to the study of section three in chapters 12 through 15. These chapters come between the sounding of the last trumpet in section two and the pouring out of the first vial of wrath in section four. There are no breaking seals, sounding trumpets, and poured out vials of wrath in these chapters. This section does not cover any part of the tribulation. Instead, it sets the stage for the final view of the tribulation in section four.

These chapters may well be considered a parenthesis, but I prefer to think of them as connecting chapters. As connecting chapters they serve as an introduction to section four.

The vision of the hundred and forty-four thousand men of Israel in Heaven reaches back to where they were sealed in section two (Revelation 7). The vision of the seven angels coming from the temple in Heaven with the vials of wrath, in Revelation 15:1, looks forward to section four where the vials of wrath will be poured out. In section four we will see the tribulation from the viewpoint of Gentile nations, and it will bring us to the Second Coming of Christ for the third and final time.

A Summary of Chapters 12-15

Chapter 12 gives a panoramic view of the conflict of the ages from the rebellion and fall of Satan to his destruction in the Battle of Armageddon. Chapter 13 pictures the rise of Antichrist and the false prophet. Chapter 14 shows the hundred and forty-four thousand redeemed Jews in Heaven, gives a vision of an angel with the everlasting Gospel to preach, announces the fall of Babylon, and gives a preview of the harvest of the earth and the Battle of Armageddon. Chapter 15 again shows the tribulation Jews in Heaven, singing a new song, and introduces the seven angels that are to pour out their vials of wrath in section four.

Contents of Chapter 12

1. The woman clothed with the sun (verses 1, 2)
2. The great red dragon (verse 3)
3. Satan's angels cast down (verse 4)
4. The man child (verse 5)
5. The flight of the woman (verse 6)
6. War in Heaven (verses 7-9)
7. Israel's enemy defeated (verse 10)
8. The Jewish victory over Satan (verse 11)
9. A blessing and a woe (verse 12)
10. Israel persecuted (verse 13)

The Woman Clothed With the Sun

1 And there appeared a great won-der in heaven; <u>a woman clothed with the sun, and the moon under her feet, and upon her head a crown of twelve stars:</u>
2 And <u>she being with child cried, travailing in birth, and pained to be de-livered.</u>

Chapter 12 opens with a vision of a woman who is about to give birth to a child. She is clothed with the sun. The moon is under her feet, and she is wearing a crown of twelve stars. The vision is called a great wonder.

There are many conjectures regarding the identity of the woman, but there is no question who she represents. The twelves stars in her crown symbolize the twelve tribes of Israel. She gives birth to the future Messiah of Israel, and, later in the chapter, she flees from Satan and hides in the wilderness. When Satan cannot defeat the woman in the wilderness he makes war with the remnant of her seed.

The sun and moon and stars speak of the heavenly origin of the woman. Using the sun and moon as types sheds light on the subject. In Gen-esis 1:16 we read, *And God made two great lights; the greater light to rule the day, and the lesser light to rule the night: he made the stars also.*

This historical account of what God did on the fourth day of creation is also a type of Christ and the church. Christ is the greater light, and the church is the lesser light. As the light of the moon is the reflected light of the sun, the church is the reflected light of Christ. Israel gave us both Christ, the greater light, and the church, the lesser light, so it is fitting that the woman representing Israel be clothed with the sun and that the moon should be under her feet.

The Great Red Dragon

3 And there appeared another wonder in heaven; and behold <u>a great red dragon, having seven heads and ten horns, and seven crowns upon his heads.</u>

In verse 3 a great red dragon with seven heads, ten horns, and seven crowns appears. His appearance in the heavens is called another wonder. In verse 9 the dragon is identified as the devil and Satan. Satan has ever been the enemy of Israel, and he will tempt and persecute the seed of Israel as long as he is free.

Many attempts have been made to explain the meaning of the seven heads, the seven crowns, and the ten horns of the dragon, but there is little agreement among those who have written on The Revelation regarding what they mean. The most that can be safely said here is that the red dragon is Satan. We must look elsewhere in The Revelation to find the meaning of the seven heads and the ten horns.

In Revelation 13:1 the beast out of the sea (Antichrist), like Satan, has seven heads and ten horns. The scarlet beast in chapter 17, that carries the harlot woman, also has seven heads and ten horns. The symbol of seven heads and ten horns appears to run in the family.

In Revelation 17:7, the mystery of the seven heads is given. An angel said to John regarding the woman on the scarlet beast, *I will tell thee the mystery of the woman, and of the beast that carrieth her, which hath the seven heads and ten horns.* In verses 9 and 10 the angel continued, *The seven heads are seven mountains, on which the woman sitteth. And there are seven kings* . . . The seven heads symbolize seven mountains. They also symbolize seven kings. The seven crowns upon the head of the dragon indicates that he will be the controlling power behind the seven kings.

We must turn to Revelation 17:12 to learn the meaning of the ten horns. There we read. *And the ten horns which thou sawest are ten kings, which have received no kingdom as yet; but receive power as kings one hour with the beast.*

The horns represent the kings that will reign over the revived Roman Empire until their kingdoms are taken over by Antichrist.

Satan's Angels Cast Down

4 And his tail drew the third part of the stars of heaven, and did cast them to the earth: and the dragon stood before the woman which was ready to be delivered, for to devour her child as soon as it was born.

Satan's tail drawing a third part of the stars in Heaven indicates that a third of the angels fell with him when he rebelled against God. The record of that fall is found in Isaiah 14 and Ezekiel 28. God's angels are beyond number, and a third of them falling indicates that Satan has many angels. Satan's angels are mentioned in Matthew 25:41; Revelation 12:7; and Revelation 12:9.

Verse 4 tells of two events that are separated by a vast amount of time. Satan and his angels fell before Adam and Eve were created. His attempt to devour the man child the woman bore did not occur until Jesus was born and he used Herod to have all the babies two years old and under slain in an effort to destroy Him.

The prediction of events in a single verse that will be fulfilled thousands of years apart is not unusual in Bible prophecy. For example, Isaiah covers the birth of Jesus and His reign as the Messiah of Israel in one verse.

For unto us a child is born, unto us a son is given: and the government shall be upon his shoulder (Isa. 9:6).

The Man Child

5 And she brought forth a man child, who was to rule all nations with a rod of iron: and her child was caught up unto God, and to his throne.

Verse 5 covers three events that are widely separated in time. The events are the birth of Jesus, the ascension of Jesus, and the kingship of Jesus. The first part of the verse was fulfilled when Jesus was born. The last part of the verse was fulfilled when He ascended back to Heaven after He arose from the dead. The middle part of the verse speaks of, *a man child, who was to rule all nations with a rod of iron:* That will be fulfilled after Jesus returns to the earth at His Second Coming.

The Flight of the Woman

6 And the woman fled into the wilderness, where she hath a place prepared of God, that they should feed her there a thousand two hundred and threescore days.

Verse 6 covers an event that will take place when the people of Israel have to flee for their lives. Midway through the tribulation, Antichrist will decide that he wants to be recognized as God and will move into the temple and demand that people worship him. The Jews will either have to worship him or flee to keep from being killed. That will mark the beginning of the last half of the tribulation.

The prophet, Daniel, predicted this event and called it the abomination of desolation (Dan. 11:31). Jesus spoke of this time and told the Jews to flee for their lives when it happened.

> *When ye therefore shall see the abomination of desolation spoken of by Daniel the prophet, stand in the holy place, (whoso readeth, let him understand:) Then let them which be in Judaea flee into the mountains (Matt. 24:15, 16).*

It is likely that many of the Jews will flee to the ancient rock city of Petra to escape death at the hands of Antichrist. There is no proof of this, but it is logical to believe that it will happen. Some reasons for believing this follow.

1. Petra is a city carved from the rock walls of canyons by the Nabataeans more than twenty-eight hundred years ago. Called "The City that Time Forgot," Petra is still there today. Armies,

time, weather, and earthquakes have been unable to destroy Petra, and it will exist as long as time shall last.

2. Petra is the most easily defended city on earth. It is located in large canyons, and the only way into them is through a narrow gorge called the Siq. The Siq is 12 to 40 feet wide. Its sides are from 200 to a 1000 feet high, and it is so narrow in places that it almost shuts out the light of the sky. A handful of men could hold the entrance of the Siq against an army.

3. Another reason the Jews may flee to Petra is that it will be a perfect bomb shelter and fall-out shelter. After about two miles, the Siq opens into a large canyon with high stone walls on either side. Carved into those walls are temples, tombs, and elaborate buildings, some of them hundreds of feet above the ground. Canyons, with cliffs on either side, lead off in several directions. These canyons also contain many rooms, temples, and buildings carved into the cliffs. These buildings are scattered over an area of 400 square miles. In the past the city may have housed no more than 30,000, but it could house a very large number of refugees.

4. Antichrist will not have control of Petra, and that will make it a logical place for the fleeing Jews to find shelter. Petra and the surround-

ing area was the ancient home of the Edomites. Antichrist will conquer many countries, but Daniel tells us that Edom will not be one of them.

> *He shall enter into the glorious land* (Palestine) *and many countries shall be overthrown: but these shall escape out of his hand, even Edom and Moab (Dan. 11:41).*

War in Heaven

> *7 And there was war in heaven: Michael and his angels fought against the dragon; and the dragon fought and his angels,*
>
> *8 And prevailed not; neither was their place found any more in heaven.*
>
> *9 And the great dragon was cast out, that old serpent, called the Devil, and Satan, which deceiveth the whole world: he was cast out into the earth, and his angels were cast out with him.*

The chapter now returns to the conflict between God and the devil. Eons ago, Satan rebelled and was cast down from his high position (Ezek. 28:17), but he remained the prince of the power of the air (Eph. 2:2).

The book of Job tells that Satan appeared before God with the sons of God (Job. 1:6). These sons of God were created angels. Even though Satan was a fallen angel, he was permitted to come before God with the other angels.

Through the centuries Satan has also been free to visit and roam the earth. He tempted Eve in the garden of Eden, and he tempted Jesus on the Mount of Temptation. Jesus told Peter that Satan desired to sift him as wheat. Paul wrote that Satan hindered him in his missionary work, and Peter wrote that Satan walks about as a roaring lion, seeking whom he may devour.

Satan is now free to move between the heavenly realm and earth as he will, but the time will come when he will be cast out of the heavens into the earth. Verses 7 through 9 tell how this will happen.

The combatants will be Michael and his angels and the dragon (Satan) and his angels. The outcome of the war is certain. Satan and his angels will be defeated and cast out of the heavens. After that his sphere of activity will be limited to the earth. He will come down to the earth with great wrath, and he will cause terrible things to happen. That will be the beginning of the end for Satan. In the next verse victory over him is proclaimed.

Israel's Enemy Defeated

10 And I heard a loud voice saying in heaven, <u>Now is come salvation, and strength, and the kingdom of our God,</u>

and the power of his Christ: for the ac-
cuser of our brethren is cast down, which
accused them before our God day and
night.

Through the centuries Satan has caused suffering and death to the people of Israel. He has turned the nations of the earth against them. He has caused them to be expelled from their homeland, and he has caused them to be persecuted and killed in many countries. Six million of them perished in Hitler's death camps during World War II.

Since May 14, 1948, when Israel declared statehood, the nation has experienced numerous wars and armed conflicts, and it continues to be under attack by terrorists who want to destroy them as a nation and as a people. Satan will continue his attempt to destroy Israel until he himself is destroyed.

The Jewish Victory Over Satan

11 And they overcame him by the
blood of the Lamb, and by the word of
their testimony; and they loved not their
lives unto the death.

In verse 11 there is a pause in the visions, and the troubled, persecuted Jews are told how they can have victory over Satan. They can overcome him by the blood of the Lamb and by their testimony. After they are saved, even in death, they will be victorious, for they will be alive in Heaven.

A Blessing and a Woe

12 Therefore <u>rejoice, ye heavens,</u> and ye that dwell in them. <u>Woe</u> to the inhabiters of the earth and of the sea! for the devil is come down unto you, having great wrath, because he knoweth that he hath but a short time.

Verse 12 opens by saying, *rejoice, ye heavens.* The heavens are told to rejoice because Satan has been cast out of them, but it is not yet time for people on earth to rejoice. The next verse announces that Satan has come down to earth in great wrath because he knows that his time is short. Satan and his angels will make life on earth so miserable that this is called the third woe.

Israel Persecuted

13 And when the dragon saw that he was cast unto the earth, <u>he persecuted the woman which brought forth the man child.</u>

Satan has persecuted the people of Israel from the beginning of their existence. After he has been cast down to the earth, he will intensify his persecution.

The Escape of the Woman

14 And to <u>the woman were given two wings of a great eagle, that she might fly into the wilderness, into her place</u>, where she is nourished for a time, and times, and half a time, from the face of the serpent.

Verse 14 tells how Israel will escape from Antichrist, and how the people will go into hiding and be nourished for the last half of the tribulation. Most likely the United States, will furnish large airliners to fly the escaping Jews from Israel to their hiding place. There they will be furnished the necessities of life for three and a half years. That will require an airlift far greater than the Berlin airlift in 1948.

Satan's Failed Tactic

15 <u>And the serpent cast out of his mouth water as a flood after the woman,</u> that he might cause her to be carried away of the flood.

16 <u>And the earth helped the woman,</u> and the earth opened her mouth, and <u>swallowed up the flood</u> which the dragon cast out of his mouth.

Satan will attack the people of Israel in their

hiding place, but his attack will not be successful. The flood of water that he will send after them is symbolic, but what it represents is clear. Satan will be unsuccessful in his attempt to destroy the Jews in their hiding place.

War With the Remnant

17 And <u>the dragon was wroth with the woman, and went to make war with the remnant of her seed, which keep the commandments of God, and have the testimony of Jesus Christ.</u>

When Satan fails to conquer the people of Israel who have fled, he will turn upon the believing remnant that did not flee. They will have little ability to defend themselves, but they will remain steadfast in their faith unto death. Most of them, perhaps all of them, will be ushered into Heaven by being martyred.

Chapter 13

Introduction to Chapter 13

*I*n the first verse of this chapter Antichrist bursts upon the scene as the beast out of the sea. The beast out of the sea will be Satan's false christ, and he will have the same identifications as Satan. As we saw in the last chapter, both Satan and the Antichrist will have seven heads and ten horns. Like Satan, Antichrist will desire to be worshiped.

In verse 11 the false prophet rises out of the earth. His mission will be to deceive people into believing that Antichrist is the real Christ. The number of the Antichrist, given in verse 18, is the great mystery of the chapter.

Contents of Chapter 13

1. The beast out of the sea (verse 1)
2. The symbols of the beast (verse 2)
3. The beast wounded and healed (verses 3, 4)
4. The last half of the tribulation (verses 5-8)
5. An appeal to the saved (verse 9)
6. Great lawlessness (verse 10)

7. The second beast arises (verses 11, 12)
8. Miracles of deception (verses 13-15)
9. The mark of the beast (verses 16, 17)
10. The number of the beast (verse 18)

The Beast Out of the Sea

1 And <u>I stood upon the sand of the sea, and saw a beast rise up out of the sea, having seven heads and ten horns, and upon his horns ten crowns,</u> and upon his heads the name of blasphemy.

The sea from which the beast will rise is a symbol of the masses of mankind. That is made clear in Revelation 17:15. There we read, . . . *The waters which thou sawest . . . are peoples, and multitudes, and nations, and tongues.*

Antichrist will fight and win several wars and negotiate treaties to his advantage as he rises to power. In time he will seize control of the governments of the entire world.

Antichrist will defeat most of the Arab nations in battle (Dan. 11:41). After that he will move the seat of his government to Jerusalem (Dan. 11:45). He will promise to defend the Jews, and, believing that he will make them safe, they will disarm. That will fulfill Ezekiel's prophecy that the time will come when one of the most heavily armed nations on earth will disarm. When Gog and his allies attack Israel their cities will be without walls or gates (Ezek. 38: 11). That is a picture of unarmed and unprotected cities.

The Symbols of the Beast

2 And the <u>beast which I saw was like</u> <u>unto a leopard, and his feet were as the</u> <u>feet of a bear, and his mouth as the</u> <u>mouth of a lion</u>: and the dragon gave him his power, and his seat, and great authority.

The vision that John saw of the beast in verse 2 is symbolic of the three empires that preceded the Roman Empire. The text says that he was like a leopard, that he had feet like a bear, and a mouth like a lion. Looking backward in time, these three animals symbolize, in reverse order, the three world empires that preceded Rome.

In Daniel 7:3-7, the prophet wrote of his vision of four beasts that symbolized past empires (including Rome) in the correct order. The lion came first, representing Babylon. The bear came second, representing Medo Persia, and the leopard came third, representing the Grecian Empire. The fourth beast, with ten horns and great iron teeth represented Rome.

Scofield has a good comment on verse 2 of this chapter of The Revelation on page 1341 of the old Scofield Bible:

The three animals, leopard, bear, and lion are found in Dan. 7:4-6 as symbols of the empires which preceded Rome, and whose characteristics all entered into the qualities of the Roman Empire; Macedonian swiftness of conquest, Persian tenacity of purpose, Babylonish voracity.

Verse 2 of this chapter gives the secret of Antichrist's power. . . . *and the dragon gave him his power, and his seat, and great authority.*

The Beast Wounded and Healed

3 And I saw <u>one of his heads as it were wounded to death</u>; <u>and his deadly wound was healed: and all the world wondered after the beast.</u>

4 <u>And they worshipped the dragon which gave power unto the beast: and they worshipped the beast</u>, saying, <u>Who is like unto the beast? who is able to make war with him?</u>

Verse 3 tells that one of the heads of the beast being wounded unto death and being healed. What this means has long been a source of controversy.

Scofield believed that the head wounded to death was the fall of the imperial government of the Roman Empire. The healing of the wound, he believed, will be the restoration of the Roman government in the last days by a federation of ten kingdoms. He says on page 1342 of the old Scofield Bible:

Fragments of the ancient Roman Empire have never ceased to exist as separate kingdoms. It was the imperial form of government which ceased; the one head wounded to death. What we have prophetically in Rev. 13:3 is the restoration of the imperial form as such through a federated empire of ten kingdoms; the head is healed, i.e. restored; there is an emperor again---the Beast.

Another suggested explanations is that Satan will let Antichrist appear to die and rise from the dead in imitation of the resurrection of Christ. This may be, for the text does not say that he died. It only says, *I saw one of his heads as it were wounded to death; and his deadly wound was healed.*

Whatever the meaning of Antichrist receiving the deadly wound and being healed, the event will turn the whole world in his favor. The last phrase in the verse 3 says, *and all the world wondered after the beast.*

Verse 4 tells us that the healing of the deadly wound will cause people to worship Satan and the beast, and it will cause them to believe that no one can defeat the beast in battle.

People will come to believe that Antichrist is the only one who can save the world from destruction by terrorists. They will never dream that he will bring the world to its greatest time of trouble.

The prophet Daniel predicted that Antichrist will be the cause of the tribulation. He foretold when the tribulation will begin, how long it will last, and that the last half of it will be the abomination of desolation.

> *And he shall confirm the covenant* (treaty) *with many for one week* (seven years); *and in the midst of the week he shall cause the sacrifice and the oblation to cease, and for the overspreading of abominations he shall make it desolate* . . . *(Dan. 9:27).*

Antichrist will appear to be the friend of Israel, and many will believe that he is their long expected Messiah. He will make a covenant with Israel for one week of years (seven years), and he will allow them to worship in the newly-built temple.

Halfway through the seven year covenant, Antichrist will expel the Jews from the temple, move into it himself, and demand to be worshiped as God. That will mark the beginning of the last three and one half years of the tribulation.

The Last Half of the Tribulation

5 And there was given unto him a mouth speaking great things and blas-

phemies; <u>and power was given unto him</u>
<u>to continue forty and two months</u> (three
and one half years).

6 <u>And he opened his mouth in blas-</u>
<u>phemy against God, to blaspheme his</u>
<u>name, and his tabernacle, and them that</u>
<u>dwell in heaven.</u>

7 <u>And it was given unto him to make</u>
<u>war with the saints, and to overcome</u>
<u>them: and power was given him over all</u>
<u>kindreds, and tongues, and nations.</u>

8 <u>And all that dwell upon the earth</u>
<u>shall worship him, whose names are not</u>
<u>written in the book of life of the Lamb</u>
slain from the foundation of the world.

After Antichrist moves into the temple he
will show his true nature. He will blaspheme the
name of God, blaspheme the tabernacle of God,
and blaspheme those who are in Heaven. He will
hate the saints on earth, make war against them,
and overcome them. He will defeat all enemies
and will come to have power over all nations.
He will be worshiped as were the god-kings of
ancient times.

In spite of his power and popular appeal
some will refuse to worship Antichrist or to receive his mark upon their foreheads or their
hands. They will not be allowed to buy or sell.
They will suffer terrible persecution, and many
of them will be killed.

An Appeal to the Saved

9 If any man have an ear, let him hear.

The same appeal that was made to the churches in the seven letters that John wrote in chapters two and three is now made to individual believers. There will be no true churches in the world during the reign of Antichrist, so the appeal will be made for individuals to listen to the leading of the Spirit. They will need the leading of the Spirit in the time when most of the world will be worshiping Satan.

Great Lawlessness

10 He that leadeth into captivity shall go into captivity: he that killeth with the sword must be killed with the sword. Here is the patience and the faith of the saints.

During the time of Antichrist's reign there will be great lawlessness. Doubtless, there will be kidnapping, raping, robbery, and murder, for Satan will be in control. The saved that are on earth during this terrible time will need the great patience and faith that are mentioned in the verse above.

The Second Beast Arises

11 And I beheld another beast coming up out of the earth; and he had two

horns like a lamb, and he spake as a
dragon.

12 And he exerciseth all the power
of the first beast before him, and causeth
the earth and them which dwell therein
to worship the first beast, whose deadly
wound was healed.

The beast out of the earth will be the third person of the evil trinity. He will look like a lamb, but he will talk like a dragon (verse 11). He is called the false prophet (Rev. 16:13b).

As the Holy Spirit testifies of Jesus, the false prophet will testify of Antichrist, but there will be a great difference. The Holy Spirit leads people to trust in Jesus and be saved. The false prophet will force people to worship Antichrist and be damned.

Miracles of Deception

13 And he doeth great wonders, so
that he maketh fire come down from
heaven on the earth in the sight of men,

14 And deceiveth them that dwell on
the earth by the means of those miracles
which he had power to do in the sight of
the beast; saying to them that dwell on
the earth, that they should make an im-
age to the beast, which had the wound
by a sword, and did live.

15 And he had power to give life unto the image of the beast, that the image of the beast should both speak, <u>and cause that as many as would not worship the image of the beast should be killed.</u>

The false prophet will be a wonder-worker and a deceiver. He will cause people to make an image of the beast, and he will give life to the image. He will demand that people worship the world's first talking idol. That will not be religion by choice. It will be religion by force. Those who refuse to worship the image of the beast will be put to death.

The Mark of the Beast

16 <u>And he causeth all, both small and great, rich and poor, free and bond, to receive a mark in their right hand, or in their foreheads:</u>

17 <u>And that no man might buy or sell, save he that had the mark,</u> or the name of the beast, or the number of his name.

The mark of the beast will be used to control all people. No one will be allowed to buy or sell without it. In our day it is easy to understand how Antichrist will put his mark on people. It is now possible for a mark to be put on the hand or the forehead of a person that can be read by scanners.

The Number of the Beast

18 Here is wisdom. Let him that hath understanding count the number of the beast: for <u>it is the number of a man; and his number is Six hundred threescore and six.</u>

There has been more speculation, and more theories about the number of the beast than anything else in the Bible. There have been almost as many attempts to count the number of the beast as there have been men who have written about the book of The Revelation.

Many prominent leaders of the past have been thought to be the Antichrist, and many ingenious schemes have been used in efforts to prove that they were. So far no one has been able to solve the mystery of the number 666.

The late Evangelist William E. Biederwolf had a good suggestion concerning the number of Antichrist. He wrote:

> Until Antichrist comes the mystery
> will not be solved, but when he comes
> believers will be able to recognize him
> by this number.

In 1946 the late Dr. M. R. De Haan, M.D., in his book, entitled *Revelation,* wrote as much as can safely be said about the number of the beast.

The number is 666, and the same verse tells us the meaning. It is the number of man. Place the emphasis in this verse on the word man. Six is the number of man. Three is the number of divinity. Here is the interpretation. The beast will be a man who claims to be God. Three sixes imply that he is a false god and a deceiver, but he is nevertheless merely a man, regardless of his claims. Seven is the number of divine perfection, and 666 is one numeral short of seven. This man of sin will reach the highest peak of power and wisdom, but he will still be merely a man.

Chapter 14

Introduction to Chapter 14

*C*hapter 14 contains eleven visions and gives a preview of the coming of the Lord and the judgments His coming will bring, including the Battle of Armageddon.

Vision one is of redeemed Israel in Heaven. Vision two is of a voice from Heaven, and the sound of harpers harping with their harps. Vision three is of the hundred and forty-four thousand singing a new song in Heaven. Vision four is of an angel preaching the everlasting Gospel. Vision five is of an angel proclaiming the fall of Babylon. Vision six is of an angel with a warning to worshipers of the beast. Vision seven is of a voice with a promise to the faithful. Vision eight is a vision of the Second Coming of Christ. Vision nine is the vision of the harvest of the redeemed. Vision ten is a vision of the final harvest of the wicked, and vision eleven is a vision of the Battle of Armageddon.

Contents of Chapter 14

1. Redeemed Israel in Heaven (verse 1)
2. A voice from Heaven (verse 2)
3. The new song (verses 3-5)
4. An angel preaching (verses 6, 7)
5. An angel's proclamation (verse 8)
6. The angel with a warning (verses 9-11)
7. Reward promised to the faithful (verses 12, 13)
8. The Second Coming (verse 14)
9. The harvest of the redeemed (verses 15, 16)
10. The harvest of the wicked (verses 17-19)
11. The Battle of Armageddon (verse 20)

Vision Number One
Redeemed of Israel in Heaven

1 And I looked, and, <u>lo, a Lamb stood on the mount Sion, and with him an hundred forty and four thousand,</u> having <u>his Father's name written in their foreheads.</u>

In vision number one the hundred and forty-four thousand are on the heavenly Mount Zion, and the Lamb of God is standing with them. They are clearly children of God, for His name is written in their foreheads. That is in contrast with the followers of the beast. They will have the mark of the beast in their right hands or upon their foreheads.

Some things on earth are copies of things that are in Heaven. Mount Zion is one of them. The earthly temple is another, for there is a temple in Heaven (Rev. 7:15; 14:15; 14:17; 15:5, 6; 16:1 and 16:17). Jerusalem is another. There is a city called New Jerusalem in Heaven (Rev. 3:12; 21:2). There is also an ark of the covenant in Heaven (Rev. 11:19).

Vision Number Two
A Voice From Heaven

2 And I heard a voice from heaven, as the voice of many waters, and as the voice of a great thunder: and I heard the voice of harpers harping with their harps:

The voice that sounded like many waters was the voice of Jesus. When John had his first vision of Jesus in chapter 1:15, he wrote that the Lord's voice sounded like many waters. In this vision he wrote that the Lord's voice sounded like many waters, then added that it also sounded like great thunder. Thunder is often mentioned in The Revelation as a symbol of power and judgment. It also has to do with the throne of God (Rev. 4:5). In Revelation 19:6 thunder is associated with praise and worship. In this vision John also heard musicians playing harps.

Vision Number Three
The New Song

3 And they sung as it were a new song before the throne, and before the

four beasts, and the elders: and <u>no man</u>
<u>could learn that song but the hundred</u>
<u>and forty and four thousand,</u> which were
redeemed from the earth.

4 These are they which were not de-
filed with women; for they are virgins.
<u>These are they which follow the Lamb</u>
<u>whithersoever he goeth. These were re-</u>
<u>deemed from among men, being the</u>
<u>firstfruits unto God and to the Lamb.</u>

5 And in their mouth was found no
guile: for they are without fault before
the throne of God.

In verse 3 we have a vision of the hundred
and forty-four thousand singing a new song in
the presence of the beasts and the elders. That
places them near the throne of God, for the beasts
and elders are always near His throne.

The new song was a song that only the hundred and forty-four thousand could sing. This
does not mean that others could not understand
the song or learn the words of the song. It does
mean that no one except the hundred and forty-
four thousand could sing the song from experience.

Not only were the hundred and forty-four
thousand redeemed, they had served God faithfully, and they had not been guilty of sexual im-
purity or spiritual fornication. These are the
firstfruits of Israel. Paul tells us that the time will

come when all Israel will be saved.

>*And so all Israel shall be saved: as it is written, There shall come out of Sion the Deliverer, and shall turn away ungodliness from Jacob (Rom. 11:26).*

Vision Number Four
An Angel Preaching

>*6 <u>And I saw another angel fly in the midst of heaven, having the everlasting gospel to preach unto them that dwell on the earth</u>, and to every nation, and kindred, and tongue, and people,*

>*7 Saying with a loud voice, Fear God, and give glory to him; for the hour of his judgment is come: and worship him that made heaven, and earth, and the sea, and the fountains of waters.*

When Antichrist has stopped the voice of every preacher, an angel will become the preacher. Mid-heaven will be his pulpit, and he will proclaim the everlasting gospel to all the nations of the earth. His message will be both an appeal and a warning. His appeal will be for men to fear God and give Him glory. The warning will be that judgment is coming.

This is the first and only account in the Bible of an angel preaching. The church will no longer be on earth. The hundred and forty-four thousand who have received the mark of God in their foreheads are in Heaven and can no longer preach, so God will use an angel to proclaim His message.

In Old Testament days God often used angels to deliver messages. When there is no one left on earth to preach, He will again use an angel to deliver his message.

Vision Number Five
An Angel's Proclamation

8 And there followed another angel, saying, Babylon is fallen, is fallen, that great city, because she made all nations drink of the wine of the wrath of her fornication.

In verse 8 another angel makes the terse announcement that Babylon has fallen, but he gives no details of the manner of its fall. He only said that it had fallen because it had contributed to the sinfulness of all nations. Babylon is a symbol of wickedness, and it is the epitome of Gentile world government and false religion.

As stated in a previous chapter, John often announces an event before it occurs, then covers it in detail in a future chapter. That is the case here. The fall of Babylon is announced in this verse, but the manner of its fall is given later.

There are two Babylons. They both fall, but

the details of their fall are not given until chapters 17 and 18. Those chapters cover the judgment of both ecclesiastical Babylon and commercial Babylon.

Babylon is first mentioned as Babel in Genesis 10:10. In verse 8 of that chapter we read of the birth of a man named Nimrod, a great grandson of Noah. Nimrod means "rebel." The Bible says he became a mighty hunter before the Lord. The rabbis called him, "A hunter of the souls of men."

Nimrod started a kingdom named Babel. Babel means "the gate to God." The Greek form of the word is Babylon, hence the city of Babylon and the country of Babylonia. Ancient Babylon was located in the land of Shinar. That country is now Iraq.

The people of this ancient city rebelled against God and attempted to make a name for themselves by building a great tower that would reach into the heavens. They said, . . . *Go to, let us build us a city and a tower whose top may reach unto heaven; and let us make us a name . . . (Gen. 11:4).*

Babylon is mentioned 260 times in the Bible, more often than any city, other than Jerusalem. It is mentioned five times in the next five chapters.

Babylon was the seat of false religion from

its beginning, and it will remain the symbol of false religion until it is destroyed.

Vision Number Six
The Angel With a Warning

9 And the third angel followed them, saying with a loud voice, If any man worship the beast and his image, and receive his mark in his forehead, or in his hand,

10 The same shall drink of the wine of the wrath of God, which is poured out without mixture into the cup of his indignation; and he shall be tormented with fire and brimstone in the presence of the holy angels, and in the presence of the Lamb:

11 And the smoke of their torment ascendeth up for ever and ever: and they have no rest day nor night, who worship the beast and his image, and whosoever receiveth the mark of his name.

A third angel appears in verse 6 and warns of punishment on all who worship the beast or his image and on all who receive his mark. The punishment will be suffering in eternal fire and brimstone.

Fire and brimstone are often mentioned in

the Bible in connection with God's punishment of sin. One example is Sodom and Gomorrah. God used fire and brimstone to destroy those cities. Brimstone has the smell of sulphur such as that which comes from a volcano.

Vision Number 7

Reward Promised to the Faithful

> *12 Here is the patience of the saints: here are they that keep the commandments of God, and the faith of Jesus.*
>
> *13 And I heard a voice from heaven saying unto me, Write, <u>Blessed are the dead which die in the Lord from henceforth: Yea, saith the Spirit, that they may rest from their labours; and their works do follow them.</u>*

The patience of the saints is mentioned in verse 12. The tribulation will be a dreadful time for those who remain faithful to God. They will need the patience of saints. They will not be allowed to buy or sell. They will be persecuted without mercy, and many, perhaps all of them, will be put to death.

Verse 13 tells us that it will be a blessing for them to die. That will be the only way they can escape the terrible things that will come upon the earth. Their works will follow them, and they will receive their rewards.

Vision Number Eight
The Second Coming of Christ

14 And I looked, and behold a white cloud, and upon the cloud one sat like unto the Son of man, having on his head a golden crown, and in his hand a sharp sickle.

The preview of the coming of Christ in this chapter is different from the vision of His coming in chapter 19, but that does not mean that the chapters describe different events.

The things that are different are the symbols. In this chapter Christ comes upon a cloud. In chapter 19 He comes riding upon a white horse. In this chapter Christ is wearing a golden crown. In chapter 19 He is wearing many crowns. In this chapter He comes with a sharp sickle to reap the harvest of the earth. In chapter 19 He comes with the armies of Heaven and defeats Antichrist with the sword of His mouth.

Vision Number Nine
The Harvest of the Redeemed

15 And another angel came out of the temple, crying with a loud voice to him that sat on the cloud, Thrust in thy sickle, and reap: for the time is come

for thee to reap; for the harvest of the
earth is ripe.
16 And he that sat on the cloud
thrust in his sickle on the earth; and the
earth was reaped.

There are two reapings in this chapter. The reaping described in verse 16 and the reaping described in verse 19 will be two different events. In verse 16 Christ is the reaper. In verse 19 an angel is the reaper. In verse 16 we are told that the earth was reaped. In verse 19 the vine of the earth was reaped and cast into the winepress of the wrath of God.

In the first reaping there will be no blood. In the second reaping there will be much blood. The first reaping will be the final harvest of saved people. They will be harvested by Christ and taken to a place of safety in Heaven.

The second reaping will be the harvest of the unsaved. As an unproductive vine is cut off and burned, they will be cut off and cast into the winepress of the wrath of God.

Vision Number Ten
The Harvest of the Wicked

17 And another angel came out of
the temple which is in heaven, he also
having a sharp sickle.
18 And another angel came out from

the altar, which had power over fire; and cried with a loud cry to him that had the sharp sickle, saying, Thrust in thy sharp sickle, and gather the clusters of the vine of the earth; for her grapes are fully ripe.

19 And the angel thrust in his sickle into the earth, and gathered the vine of the earth, and cast it into the great winepress of the wrath of God.

There are two different angels in verses 17 and 18. The first angel will come out of the temple in Heaven. The second angel will come from the altar. In Revelation 8:5 we learn that the altar can be an altar of judgment. The second angel will tell the first angel to reap the final harvest of the wicked who were yet in the world.

God has had a controversy with the nations through many centuries, and at last His wrath is going to be poured out upon them. The prophet Jeremiah wrote of that time . . . *the Lord hath a controversy with the nations, he will plead with all flesh; he will give them that are wicked to the sword, saith the Lord (Jer. 25:31).*

Through the centuries the wrath of God has been held back by the mercy of God, as a dam holds back the waters of a great river. When a dam in the river breaks the results are catastrophic. At the end of the age the dam of God's mercy will restrain His wrath no longer, and the harvest of the wicked will come.

Vision Number Eleven
The Battle of Armageddon

20 And the winepress was trodden without the city, and blood came out of the winepress, even unto the horse bridles, by the space of a thousand and six hundred furlongs.

Verse 20 gives a preview of the Battle of Armageddon. Juice flowing from crushed grapes in a winepress is used as a symbol of the blood that will flow from the bodies of slain men in the greatest battle of all time. The text says that blood will reach to the bridles of horses. If that means the blood will be bridle deep, the horses will be swimming in blood. If it means that blood will splatter to the horse's bridles, the ground will be covered with blood. In either case it means that multitudes of men will be slain in the battle.

The blood from the slain of that battle will reach sixteen hundred furlongs which is approximately 183 miles. That means that the battle will reach from Megiddo to the ancient land of Edom. This will be the final harvest of a wicked world that has rejected Jesus and served Satan.

The actual account of the battle is not given until chapter 19. The battle will occur when Jesus returns to the earth as King of kings and Lord of lords. At that time Antichrist will bring together the armies of the earth to fight against the armies of Heaven, and he and his armies will be defeated. That will be a fitting conclusion to the conflict of the ages.

Chapter 14 gives a preview of the Battle of Armageddon. Chapter 15, the last chapter in this section, will set the stage for section four, and it will take us through the tribulation and to the Second Coming of Christ for the third and final time.

Chapter 15

Introduction to Chapter 15

C hapter 15 is the last of the connecting chapters. The first verse introduces the seven angels that are to pour out the seven vials of wrath, but they do not pour out any vials of wrath in this chapter. This chapter sets the stage for the pouring out of the vials of wrath in chapter 16.

Chapter 16 will mark the beginning of section four. In it we will start through the tribulation for the third and final time. This time it will be from the viewpoint of the Gentiles, and it will show how the tribulation will affect apostate religion and Gentile world governments.

We are not finished with the hundred and forty-four thousand. In verses 2 through 5 we will again see them in Heaven.

In verse 6 John tells us that seven angels, beautifully arrayed in white linen and wearing golden girdles, will come from the temple. In verse 7 he tells us that one of the four beasts will give seven golden vials full of the wrath of God to the seven angels. Verse 8 tells us that the temple in Heaven will be closed until the vials of wrath are poured out.

Contents of Chapter 15

1. A sign in Heaven (verse 1)
2. A sea of glass (verse 2)
3. The song of Moses and the Lamb (verse 3)
4. The message of the song (verse 4)
5. The temple and the tabernacle (verse 5)
6. Seven angels with seven plagues (verses 6, 7)
7. God's awesome presence (verse 8)

A Sign in Heaven

1 And I saw <u>another sign in heaven, great and marvellous,</u> seven angels having the seven last plagues; for in them is filled up the wrath of God.

John's first vision of the seven angels in Heaven is called great and marvelous. That may be because of the appearance of the angels, as given in verse 6, or it may be because of the golden vials of the wrath of God that were given to them to pour out.

The Sea of Glass

2 And <u>I saw as it were a sea of glass mingled with fire: and them that had gotten the victory over the beast,</u> and over his image, and over his mark, and over

*the number of his name, stand on the
sea of glass, having the harps of God.*

In verse 2 John is given another heavenly vision. The best he could do in describing what he saw was to say that it looked like a sea of glass mingled with fire. Only in eternity will we be able to comprehend the wonders that God has prepared for those who love Him.

John saw those who had gained the victory over Antichrist standing on the sea of glass. The same sea is mentioned in verse 6 of chapter 4. There we are told that the sea of glass is before the throne of God. Chapter 4 pictures the rapture of the church, and in verse 10 it tells of the church falling down to worship God and casting their crowns before His throne.

The sea of glass appears to be a sea of victory. Those who are standing on the sea of glass, holding the harps of God, had gained the victory over Antichrist. They had refused to worship the image that the false prophet had made, and they had refused to receive the mark of the beast in their hands or their foreheads. They may have gained the final victory by being killed, for they are now in glory.

The Song of Moses and the Lamb

*3 And they sing the song of Moses
the servant of God, and the song of the
Lamb, saying, Great and marvellous are*

thy works, Lord God Almighty; just and
true are thy ways, thou King of saints.

The raptured church gave praise to God in chapter 4, but they did not sing about Moses. In this chapter we have Jewish believers, and they sing about Moses and the Lamb. They go back to Moses for their roots, and, now that they have believed on the Lamb of God, they can sing about Moses and the Lamb. This song reminds us that the law came by Moses and grace came by Jesus Christ (John 1:17).

The Message of the Song

4 Who shall not fear thee, O Lord,
and glorify thy name? for thou only art
holy: for all nations shall come and wor-
ship before thee; for thy judgments are
made manifest.

The song is a call to repentance. *Who shall not fear thee, O Lord?* It is a call to praise. *For thou only art holy; for all nations shall come and worship before thee.* It is a warning of judgments to come. *For thy judgments are made manifest.*

This is not the final judgment. The final judgment is the judgment of the wicked dead before the great white throne of God. The judgments in this chapter will come upon the earth during the tribulation.

The Temple and the Tabernacle

5 And after that I looked, and, behold, the temple of the tabernacle of the testimony in heaven was opened:

The tabernacle on earth was called the tabernacle of testimony (Ex. 38:21). The ark of the covenant was placed in the tabernacle, and the tables of testimony (the ten commandments) were placed in it (Deut. 10:5). Also, the tabernacle bore witness to the presence of God, for His presence was above the mercy seat of the ark. For these reasons the tabernacle was called the tabernacle of testimony.

After the temple was built, the ark of the covenant was paced in it, and as God's presence had been in the tabernacle, His presence was in the temple.

Seven Angels with Seven Plagues

6 And <u>the seven angels came out of the temple, having the seven plagues, clothed in pure and white linen, and having their breasts girded with golden girdles.</u>

7 And <u>one of the four beasts gave unto the seven angels seven golden vials full of the wrath of God,</u> who liveth for ever and ever.

In verses 6 and 7 the seven angels, with the

seven last plagues, are mentioned for the second time in the chapter. This time they are described, but we are not told why they are clothed in white linen or why they are wearing golden girdles. We are told however that one of the beasts gave the angels the seven golden vials full of the wrath of God. Men have rebelled against God through all the ages, and at last the time of reckoning has come.

God's Awesome Presence

8 *And the temple was filled with smoke from the glory of God, and from his power; and no man was able to enter into the temple, till the seven plagues of the seven angels were fulfilled.*

Verse 8 says that the temple was filled with smoke. This is the temple in Heaven. God's presence is sometimes manifested by smoke. When God came down upon Mount Sinai to meet with Moses, the mountain was covered with smoke, as the smoke of a furnace, and the mountain quaked. The smoke and the shaking of the mountain were evidences of God's awesome power (Ex. 19:18).

God's presence in judgment is also indicated by smoke. This will be true at the time of the Lord's Second Coming, for He will come to defeat Satan and to judge the wicked. Joel wrote of that day:

And I will shew wonders in the heavens and in the earth, blood, and fire, and pillars of smoke. The sun shall be turned into darkness, and the moon into blood, before the great and the terrible day of the LORD come (Joel 2:30-31).

The last part of verse 8 tells us that all activity in the temple in Heaven will be suspended until the seven angels have poured out the seven vials of wrath upon the earth. The stage is now set for the beginning of the great tribulation that will be covered for the third time.

Chapter 16

Introduction to Chapter 16

*A*s stated earlier, chapter 16 brings us to the beginning of section four. The imagery of the chapter is of seven angels with seven vials of the wrath of God. The chapter tells where each vial will be poured out and describes the judgments that will follow.

The pouring out of the first vial will start the tribulation from the Gentile viewpoint, and the pouring out of the remaining vials will bring us to the Second Coming of Christ for the third and final time.

After the pouring out of the sixth vial, in verse 12, verse 13 predicts the Battle of Armageddon. The final vial is poured out in verse 17, and the remaining verses give the details of the judgment that will follow.

It remains for chapters 17 through 19 to give the details of the judgment of ecclesiastical and commercial Babylon, the marriage of the Lamb, the Second Coming, and the Battle of Armageddon.

Contents of Chapter 16

1. The command given the angels (verse 1)
2. The first vial poured out (verse 2)
3. The second vial poured out (verse 3)
4. The third vial poured out (verse 4)
5. The angel of the waters (verse 5, 6)
6. The voice from the altar (verse 7)
7. The fourth vial poured out (verses 8, 9)
8. The fifth vial poured out (verses 10, 11)
9. The sixth vial poured out (verse 12)
10. Frog-like spirits (verses 13, 14)
11. The promise of Christ's coming (verse 15)
12. Armageddon foretold (verse 16)
13. The seventh vial poured out (verses 17, 18)
14. The judgment of Jerusalem (verse 19)
15. Results of the earthquake (verse 20)
16. Earth's greatest hailstorm (verse 21)

The Command to the Angels

1 And I heard a great voice out of the temple saying to the seven angels, Go your ways, and <u>pour out the vials of the wrath of God upon the earth.</u>

In verse 1 the command is given for the seven angels to pour out the seven vials of wrath upon the earth. The judgments that follow the pouring out of the vials give further evidence that The Revelation contains three views of the tribulation instead of one.

The pouring out of the vials of wrath closely parallel the sounding of the seven trumpets in chapters 8, 9, and 11. It is evident that the sounding of the seven trumpets and the pouring out of the seven vials symbolize the same events. The seven parallels are listed below.

The First Vial Poured Out

2 And the first went, and <u>poured out his vial upon the earth;</u> and <u>there fell a noisome and grievous sore upon the men which had the mark of the beast,</u> and upon them which worshipped his image.

The sounding of the first trumpet and the pouring out of the first vial will both bring judgment upon living things on the earth. The sounding of the first trumpet will cause a third part of the trees and a third part of the grass to die (Rev. 8:7). The pouring out of the first vial will bring judgment upon men who have received the mark of the beast (Rev. 16:2).

The Second Vial Poured Out

3 And <u>the second angel poured out his vial upon the sea;</u> and it became as the blood of a dead man: and every living soul died in the sea.

The sounding of the second trumpet and the pouring out of the second vial will both bring judgment upon the sea (Rev. 8:8, 9 and 16:3). In both instances the sea will become as blood. It is evident that they symbolize the same event.

The Third Vial Poured Out

4 And <u>the third angel poured out his</u>

vial upon the rivers and fountains of wa-
ters; and they became blood.

The sounding of the third trumpet and the pouring out of the third vial will both bring judgment upon the rivers and fountains of water (Rev. 8:10, 11 and 16:4).

The Angel of the Waters

5 *And I heard the angel of the wa-*
ters say, Thou art righteous, O Lord,
which art, and wast, and shalt be, be-
cause thou hast judged thus.

6 *For they have shed the blood of*
saints and prophets, and thou hast given
them blood to drink; for they are wor-
thy.

God has angels that are assigned special tasks. For example, there are angels in charge of the waters (verse 5), angels in charge of the wind (Rev. 7:1), and angels that have power over fire (Rev. 14:18).

In verse 6 the angel of the waters declares that turning the rivers and fountains of water to blood will be just punishment for whose who have killed saints and prophets.

The Voice From the Altar

7 *And I heard another out of the al-*
tar say, Even so, Lord God Almighty,
true and righteous are thy judgments.

The voice of an unknown angel from the altar affirms that the punishment of those who have martyred saints is just. The God who notes the falling of a sparrow does not take lightly the deaths of His children.

The Fourth Vial Poured Out

8 And <u>the fourth angel poured out his vial upon the sun;</u> and power was given unto him to scorch men with fire.

9 <u>And men were scorched with great heat,</u> and blasphemed the name of God, which hath power over these plagues: <u>and they repented not to give him glory.</u>

The sounding of the fourth trumpet and the pouring out of the fourth vial will both affect the sun, though the details of what will happen are different (Rev. 8:12 and 16:8).

Verse 9 tells us that judgments upon rebellious men will not cause them to repent. Men who refuse to respond to God's grace will not respond when they are punished.

The Fifth Vial Poured Out

10 And <u>the fifth angel poured out his vial upon the seat of the beast; and his kingdom was full of darkness;</u> and they gnawed their tongues for pain,

11 <u>And blasphemed the God of heaven</u> because of their pains and their *sores, and repented not of their deeds.*

The sounding of the fifth trumpet and the pouring out of the fifth vial will both cause darkness (Rev. 9:1, 2 and 16:10).

The judgment of the fifth vial will be directed against the government of Antichrist, and his kingdom will be full of darkness. The people of his government will not know where to turn, and in their desperation they will blaspheme God.

The Sixth Vial Poured Out

12 And the sixth angel poured out his vial upon the great river Euphrates; and the water thereof was dried up, that the way of the kings of the east might be prepared.

The sounding of the sixth trumpet and the pouring out of the sixth vial will both affect the River Euphrates (Rev. 9:13, 14 and 16:12).

The drying up of the river Euphrates is symbolic. Its purpose is to show that mighty armies from the east will come through the country of ancient Babylonia (now Iraq) to participate in the Battle of Armageddon.

The population of the world is now over 6 billion, and two thirds of the people on earth now live in the far east. It is from that region that an army of 200 million will come to fight the armies of Heaven at the time of Christ's Second Coming (Rev. 9:16).

There follows a pause in the account of the pouring out of the vials of wrath. During the pause the veil that separates the physical world and the spirit world is pulled aside to show how Satan will use demon spirits in the end-time battle.

Frog-Like Spirits

13 And I saw three unclean spirits like frogs come out of the mouth of the dragon, and out of the mouth of the beast, and out of the mouth of the false prophet.

14 For they are the spirits of devils, working miracles, which go forth unto the kings of the earth and of the whole world, to gather them to the battle of that great day of God Almighty.

John saw three unclean spirits that were like frogs come out of the mouths of Satan, out of the mouth of the Antichrist, and out of the mouth of the false prophet. They were not frogs. They only looked like frogs. These loathsome, frog-like creatures are symbols of the wicked spirits that Satan controls.

Verse 14 tells us that these creatures are the spirits of devils, and that they will go forth unto the kings of the whole world to gather them to the battle of the great day of God Almighty.

The kings that will serve under Antichrist

will be demon possessed, and the demons that possess them will gather them and their armies to fight in the Battle of Armageddon. These demon possessed kings will believe that they can defeat the King of kings, just as Satan believed when he fell that he could exalt his throne above the stars of God (Isa. 14:13, 14).

The Promise of Christ's Coming

15 Behold, <u>I come as a thief.</u> Blessed is he that watcheth, and keepeth his garments, lest he walk naked, and they see his shame.

In the midst of the predictions of doom and destruction, we have the Lord's assurance that He will come again. The promise of Christ's Second Coming is given immediately after the dreadful picture of demon possessed armies gathering to fight against Him and His army. The verse says that Christ will come as a thief. That means that Antichrist will be caught by surprise when Christ and the armies of Heaven appear. The verse closes with a promise of blessing to those who are living for God at the time of Christ's Second Coming.

Armageddon Foretold

16 And he gathered them together into a place called in the Hebrew tongue Armageddon.

Verse 16 announces the Battle of Armageddon, but it does not describe the battle nor give the outcome. The details of the battle and the results are given in Revelation 19:11-21.

The Seventh Vial Poured Out

17 And <u>the seventh angel poured out his vial into the air; and there came a great voice out of the temple of heaven, from the throne, saying, It is done.</u>

18 And <u>there were voices, and thunders, and lightnings; and there was a great earthquake</u>, such as was not since men were upon the earth, so mighty an earthquake, and so great.

The parallel between the sounding of the seventh trumpet and the pouring out of the seventh vial of wrath continues. After both the sounding of the seventh trumpet and the pouring out of the seventh vial there will be thunder and lightning, and an earthquake (Rev. 11:19 and 16:18).

After the sounding of the seventh trumpet, there were great voices in Heaven, saying . . . *The kingdoms of this world are become the kingdoms of our Lord, and of his Christ; and he shall reign for ever and ever (Rev. 11:15).* That says clearly that Christ had taken possession of the kingdoms of the world.

In this chapter, the terse statement, *<u>It is done,</u>*

at the end of verse 17, brings us to the end of the pouring out of vials of wrath, but several judgments are yet to come, and they will take us to the Second Coming of Christ and the Battle of Armageddon in chapter 19.

Verse 18 of our present chapter tells of the greatest earthquake of all time. *. . .and there was a great earthquake, such as was not since men were upon the earth, so mighty an earthquake, and so great.*

The parallels continue. An earthquake followed the sounding of the seventh trumpet (Rev. 11:19).

The Judgment of Jerusalem

19 And the great city was divided into three parts, and the cities of the nations fell: and great Babylon came in remembrance before God, to give unto her the cup of the wine of the fierceness of his wrath.

The great city mentioned in verse 19 is Jerusalem. In Revelation 11:8 Jerusalem is called, *. . . the great city, which spiritually is called Sodom and Egypt, where our Lord was crucified.*

Jerusalem is called great because of its history as the political and religious capitol of the Jews and because it gave birth to Christianity.

The cities of the nations will include many cities, worldwide. Verse 19 also tells us that great Babylon will come into remembrance. At last the wicked city will be judged.

There are three Babylons in the Bible. They are historical Babylon, ecclesiastical Babylon, and the rebuilt city of Babylon. There is considerable evidence that the ancient city of Babylon will be rebuilt in the last days. Some of the evidences are given in chapter 18.

Results of the Greatest Earthquake

20 And every island fled away, and the mountains were not found.

Verse 18 predicts this great earthquake. Verse 19 predicts that it will divide Jerusalem into three parts and that the cities of the nations will fall, and verse 20 says that the islands and mountains will be destroyed. There are more judgments to follow.

Earth's Greatest Hailstorm

21 And there fell upon men a great hail out of heaven, every stone about the weight of a talent: and men blasphemed God because of the plague of the hail; for the plague thereof was exceeding great.

Never has there been such a storm of hail as the one described in verse 21. The hailstones will not be made up of large and small stones as usual. They will all be large. The hailstones described in verse 21 will be 90 times heavier than any that have ever fallen upon the earth. Each hailstone will weigh 56 pounds.

Hailstones of that size will destroy roofs on buildings, demolish automobiles, and kill all the people and animals that are in the open. This will be one of the worst judgments that will come upon the earth during the tribulation.

Again, men will not repent. The earthquake and the storm of hail will only make them rebel and blaspheme God. Through the centuries God has reached out to men in mercy, grace, and love, but there have always been those who refused to respond.

Men who are on earth in the last days will be no different. They will blame God for their troubles, blaspheme His name, and continue in their sins. For that reason they will have to endure the final storms, earthquakes, and troubles that will come upon the earth. After that they will be judged and sentenced to hell forever.

Chapter 17

Introduction to Chapter 17

*T*he first seven verses of chapter 17 are about a harlot woman upon a scarlet beast. She is described in detail, and her judgment is predicted. The woman is the symbol of ecclesiastical Babylon. As such, she represents everything that is wrong about false religion.

Verses 8 through 13 are about Antichrist and the kings of the end time. Verse 14 predicts the Battle of Armageddon, and the remaining verses are about the harlot woman and her destruction. Chapter 18 is about the city of Babylon and the corrupt Gentile world system of government it represents.

The ancient city of Babylon has been in ruins for centuries, but the false religion it fostered has survived. Using the symbol of the great whore riding upon a scarlet beast, chapter 17 tells what ecclesiastical Babylon will be like in the last days.

According to ancient records, Nimrod, the founder of the city, had a wife named Semiramis.

She founded the Babylonian mystery religion and was the first high priestess of the cult that was Satan's false religion.

Satan knew that the seed of woman would be virgin born, and that He would be crucified and would rise from the dead. In an effort to make his false religion seem legitimate, he caused Semiramis to say that her son (Tammuz) had been miraculously conceived, had been killed by a wild beast, and had risen from the dead.

The ancient city of Babylon was located on the east bank of the Euphrates River, about 50 miles south of present day Bagdad. In 450 B.C. the Greek historian, Herodotus, wrote that the city was 14 miles square. According to Herodotus the wall around the city was 56 miles long, 80 feet thick, and 320 feet high. A water-filled moat surrounded the city, and 100 gates of iron and brass were in the wall. The top of the wall was wide enough for four chariots to drive around it abreast. The river Euphrates ran through the city, and the hanging gardens that Nebuchadnezzar built for his queen were one of the seven wonders of the ancient world.

It is likely that Herodotus exaggerated or that he was not well informed about the size of the city. The British historian, Gibbon, stated that Herodotus may have never set foot in Babylon. Excavations in recent times have revealed that the city was probably not more that 10 miles square, and the height of the wall may have been no more than 100 feet. Even so, Babylon was an imposing city for that day.

Contents of Chapter 17

Judgment Proclaimed

1 And there came one of the seven angels which had the seven vials, and talked with me, saying unto me, Come hither: I will shew unto thee the judgment of the great whore that sitteth upon many waters:

2 With whom the kings of the earth have committed fornication, and the inhabitants of the earth have been made drunk with the wine of her fornication.

In verse 1 of this chapter, one of the seven angels that came to John in chapter 16 identified Babylon as the great whore that sitteth upon many waters. In verse 15 we are told that the waters where the whore sitteth are peoples and multitudes and nations. The whore represents a false religion that has endured and will influence much of the religious world in the last days.

Much is said in The Revelation about the destruction of Babylon. In Revelation 14:8 it is announced that *Babylon is fallen, is fallen.* In Revelation 16:19 we are told that, *great Babylon came in remembrance before God.* In Revelation 18:2 an angel cried mightily with a strong voice, *Babylon the great is fallen is fallen.* In Revelation 18:21 we read, *Thus with violence shall that great city Babylon be thrown down, and shall be found no more at all.*

The Vision of the Scarlet Beast

3 So he carried me away in the spirit into the wilderness: and <u>I saw a woman sit upon a scarlet coloured beast,</u> full of names of blasphemy, <u>having seven heads and ten horns.</u>

The scarlet beast that John saw the woman riding is Antichrist, the beast that rose out of the sea in chapter 13. This beast has the same identification, as the one that rose out of the sea i.e., seven heads and ten horns. Antichrist will support the harlot woman as long as she is useful to him.

The Woman Described

4 And the woman was arrayed in purple and scarlet colour, and decked with gold and precious stones and pearls, having a golden cup in her hand full of abominations and filthiness of her fornication:

The woman John saw was arrayed in purple and scarlet and decked with gold, precious stones, and pearls. The purple and scarlet garments are the colors of royalty. The gold and precious stones speak of her wealth. The golden cup in her hand speaks of her sins of spiritual fornication.

The Name of the Harlot

5 And upon her forehead was a name written, MYSTERY, BABYLON THE GREAT, THE MOTHER OF HAR-LOTS AND ABOMINATIONS OF THE EARTH.

The names of the harlot are not names that she would have chosen. She would never have called herself the mother of harlots or the abomination of the earth. The names were given to her to show her wickedness and God's contempt for her.

The false religion promoted by the woman

is based upon superstition and shrouded in mystery. The mystery religion she fostered will continue until Antichrist and his puppet kings grow weary of it and destroy the harlot woman that promotes it.

Many false religions have grown out of the union of the original Babylonian cult and the corrupt state church of the Roman Empire.

Wicked practices grow out of false religion, and they become worse with each passing generation. The harlot woman, riding upon the back of Antichrist, will promote great wickedness in the earth in the last days.

End-Time Martyrs

6 And I saw the woman drunken with the blood of the <u>saints, and with the blood of the martyrs of Jesus:</u> and when I saw her, I wondered with great admiration.

Verse 6 tells us that the woman was drunken with the blood of saints and martyrs. Saints become martyrs when they die for their faith. Throughout the history of the world false religions have been responsible for the deaths of many Christians.

The Identity of the Beast

7 And the angel said unto me, Wherefore didst thou marvel? <u>I will tell</u>

thee the mystery of the woman, and of
the beast that carrieth her, which hath
the seven heads and ten horns.

8 The beast that thou sawest was,
and is not; and shall ascend out of the
bottomless pit, and go into perdition:
and they that dwell on the earth shall
wonder, whose names were not written
in the book of life from the foundation
of the world, when they behold the beast
that was, and is not, and yet is.

There are several evidences that the beast mentioned in verse 8 as the symbol of Antichrist will be Judas Iscariot returned from the dead. Following are some of the evidences.

Both Judas and Antichrist are called, "The son of perdition." Jesus called Judas the son of perdition.

. . . those that thou gavest me I have
kept, and none of them is lost, but the son
of perdition; that the scripture might be
fulfilled (John 17:12).

The Apostle Paul called the Antichrist the son of perdition.

Let no man deceive you by any means:
for that day shall not come, except there
come a falling away first, and that man
of sin be revealed, the son of perdition (2
Thess. 2:3).

Jesus said that Judas was a devil.

Jesus answered them, Have not I chosen you twelve, and <u>one of you is a devil?</u> He spake of Judas Iscariot the son of Simon: for he it was that should betray him . . . (John 6:70, 71). In the original Greek, this verse says, *of you one a devil is.*

Judas was possessed by Satan. In Luke 22:3, we read: *Then entered Satan into Judas . . .* Many have been possessed by demons, but Judas was the only one ever possessed by Satan.

When Judas died he went to his own place.

. . . Judas by transgression fell, <u>that he might go to his own place</u> (Acts 1:25).

Hell was created for the devil and his angels, so Judas, being a devil, went to his own place in hell (Matt. 25:41).

Judas fits the picture. Verse 8 says that *he was and he is not and yet is.*

Judas was alive on the earth. He died and was not. He was a devil, and he went into the pit. He will still be devil possessed when he comes out of the pit to live again as the Antichrist.

The Seven Heads Explained

9 And here is the mind which hath wisdom. <u>The seven heads are seven mountains</u>, on which the woman sitteth.

The seven heads of the beast have a dual meaning. They symbolize both seven kings and seven mountains. In Revelation 12:3 and 13:1 we are told that the beast had seven heads, and in Revelation 17:9 we read that the seven heads are seven mountains.

The crowns represent kings, and the mountains indicate a location. The location is Rome, the city on seven hills. The union of the Babylonian false religion and the corrupt church of Rome created a religious hierarchy that exerted power over the kings of the earth for centuries.

The Seven Kings

10 <u>And there are seven kings</u>: five are fallen, and one is, and the other is not yet come; and when he cometh, he must continue a short space.

There has been much speculation concerning the identity of the five fallen kings, the one remaining king, and the seventh king that will rule for a brief time.

As stated in an earlier chapter, the four kingdoms represented by the great image in Nebuchadnezzar's dream (Daniel 2) are Babylon, Medo-Persia, Greece, and Rome. Some scholars have suggested that Egypt and Assyria may be the other two kingdoms. The Roman ruler, Domitian, was reigning when John wrote The Revelation, so he may be king number six instead.

The verse also tells us that king number seven will only be in power for a short time, but it gives no hint of his identity. We must turn to the book of Daniel for that information. Daniel tells us that an unnamed king, who will be a raiser of taxes, will be in power for a short time before king number 8 comes to power.

> *Then shall stand up in his estate a raiser of taxes in the glory of the kingdom: but within few days he shall be destroyed, neither in anger, nor in battle.*
>
> *And in his estate shall stand up a vile person, to whom they shall not give the honour of the kingdom: but he shall come in peaceably and obtain the kingdom by flatteries (Dan. 11:20, 21).*

The Eighth King

11 And the beast that was, and is not, even he is the eighth, and is of the seven, and goeth into perdition.

The text says that Antichrist will be the eighth king, but he is of the seven. Antichrist will take over the kingdom from king number seven, and that will make him number eight.

The Ten Horns Identified

12 And the ten horns which thou sawest are ten kings, which have re-

ceived no kingdom as yet; but receive
power as kings one hour with the beast.
     13 These have one mind, and shall
give their power and strength unto the
beast.

The ten horns of the beast symbolize the ten kings that will govern the revived Roman Empire for a short time before Antichrist comes to power. Antichrist will defeat three of these kings in battle, and God will put it in the hearts of the remaining seven kings to give the kingdom to him (Dan. 11:21).

The rapture will prepare the way for the ten kings to come to power. So many people will be taken from the earth by the rapture that the governments of the world will be bankrupt. New governments will be formed and ten kings will eventually come to power.

A Future Prediction

     14 These shall make war with the
Lamb, and the Lamb shall overcome
them: for he is Lord of lords, and King
of kings: and they that are with him are
called, and chosen, and faithful.

Verse 14 looks forward to the Second Coming of Christ and the Battle of Armageddon. The Lamb that was led to the slaughter and was dumb before His shearers (Isa. 53:7) will be the King of kings and Lord of lords when He comes again as foretold in chapter 19.

Antichrist and his puppet kings will make the fatal mistake of making war with Christ and His army. Christ will defeat Antichrist and he and his false prophet will be cast into the lake of fire and brimstone.

The Meaning of the Waters

15 And he saith unto me, <u>The waters</u> which thou sawest, <u>where the whore sitteth, are peoples, and multitudes, and nations, and tongues.</u>

As stated earlier, verse 15 explains the meaning of the waters where the whore is sitting.

As the symbol of ecclesiastical Babylon the whore has had great influence over the nations in the past, and she will have great influence over the nations in the last days.

Verse 18 tells us that she has reigned over the kings of the earth. The only religion that ever reigned over the kings of the earth was the Catholic church with its headquarters in Rome.

The Destruction of the Whore

16 And <u>the ten horns</u> which thou sawest upon the beast, <u>these shall hate the whore, and shall make her desolate and naked, and shall eat her flesh, and burn her with fire.</u>

Verse 16 gives proof that ecclesiastical

Babylon and commercial Babylon are not the same. In this chapter the ten kings hate ecclesiastical Babylon and rejoice when she is destroyed. There will be no lamenting over the destruction of the corrupt religious system that she represents, but when commercial Babylon is destroyed the kings will lament over her.

> *And the kings of the earth . . . shall bewail her, and lament for her, when they see the smoke of her burning (Rev. 18:9).*

God is in Control

> *17 For God hath put in their hearts to fulfil his will, and to agree, and give their kingdom unto the beast, until the words of God shall be fulfilled.*

God will put it in the hearts of the ruling kings to let Antichrist come to power to fulfill His purpose. Satan will again be deceived. He will believe that he can rule the world through Antichrist, and that he can defeat the King of kings in the last war.

Babylon Identified

> *18 And the woman which thou sawest is that great city, which reigneth over the kings of the earth.*

The roots of western civilization have their origin in Rome, and the remnants of the Roman government have never ceased to exist. The foundation of many western languages are found in Latin, the Roman language. Even our calendar is based on the calendar that was implemented by Julius Caesar in 46-45 B.C.

Antichrist will use the religious system that is controlled by the great whore on his rise to power. Apparently this relationship will continue until mid-tribulation when Antichrist and his puppet kings will grow weary of the whore and destroy her.

After the whore is destroyed Antichrist will move into the rebuilt Jewish temple and declare that he is God, and that will mark the beginning of the last half of the tribulation.

> *Let no man deceive you by any means: for that day shall not come, except there come a falling away first, and that man of sin be revealed, the son of perdition:*
> *Who opposeth and exalteth himself above all that is called God, or that is worshipped; so that he as God sitteth in the temple of God, shewing himself that he is God (2 Thess. 2:3, 4).*

Jesus called this move by Antichrist the abomination of desolation spoken by Daniel the prophet (Matt. 24:15). The references in Daniel are found in Dan. 9:27 and 12:11.

When Antichrist turns against the Jews, expels them from the temple, moves into the temple, and demands that he be worshiped as god. That will mark the beginning of the time that is called the time of Jacob's trouble.

Alas! for that day is great, so that none is like it: it is even the time of Jacob's trouble; but he shall be saved out of it (Jer. 30:7).

As noted earlier, the Jews will flee for their lives, and will, most likely, find shelter in the ancient rock-hewn city of Petra.

Already the nation of Israel is in great trouble. Militant Muslims in several nations are advocating the destruction of the Jewish state. As this is being written, President Bashar Al-Asad of Iran, is attempting to develop nuclear bombs, and he has stated that Israel should be wiped off the face of the map. There is no hope that even a change of leadership will change the goal of militant Muslims in Syria and other militant Arab States.

It may only be a short time until terrorists have nuclear bombs. When they have them the United States will not be safe, nor will any other western nation. The agenda of militant Muslims is to gain control of all nations, govern them under Moslem law, and put to death all who refuse to become Muslims.

We live in frightful times. It is possible for an atomic war to kill much of the population of the world and destroy civilization as we know it, but we need not despair. Jesus foresaw our day and said that following the tribulation the days would be shortened so that all flesh would not be destroyed.

> *For then shall be great tribulation, such as was not since the beginning of the world to this time, no, nor ever shall be. And except those days should be shortened, there should no flesh be saved: but for the elect's sake those days shall be shortened (Matt. 24:21, 22).*

For those who have no faith, this is a hopeless hour, but for the children of God it is an exciting hour. The coming of the Lord is drawing near, and when He comes He will take charge and bring order to a world that Satan has brought to the verge of destruction.

Chapter 18

Introduction to Chapter 18

*O*nce again John begins a chapter with the phrase, *after these things.* The destruction of ecclesiastical Babylon is finished, and this chapter will give the details of the destruction of commercial Babylon.

Ecclesiastical Babylon is symbolic, and some believe that commercial Babylon is symbolic as well. They believe that the fall of Babylon will not be the fall of a literal city but the collapse of the political and commercial systems of the world, but that position is not supported in the Bible.

More than 700 years before the birth of Christ, Isaiah prophesied that Babylon will be destroyed in the last days. <u>The city will have to be rebuilt before it can be destroyed.</u>

Some believe that Isaiah's prediction of the destruction of Babylon was fulfilled in the past, but according to his prophecy it will be fulfilled in the future.

The 13th chapter of Isaiah begins with the words, *The burden of Babylon*. That tells what the chapter is about. In the chapter Isaiah predicted the destruction of Babylon and said it would be destroyed when the day of the Lord was at hand. The day of the Lord is the day of Christ's Second Coming. About that day Isaiah wrote:

> *Howl ye; for the day of the LORD is at hand; it shall come as a destruction from the Almighty (Isa. 13:6).*

Isaiah continues:

> *For the stars of heaven and the constellations thereof shall not give their light: the sun shall be darkened in his going forth, and the moon shall not cause her light to shine (Isa. 13:10).*

The above verse dates the fulfillment of Isaiah's prophecy. He predicated that the sun will be darkened and the moon will not give light. Jesus said this will happen immediately after the tribulation and before the Second Coming. His prediction follows.

> *Immediately after the tribulation of those days shall the sun be darkened, and the moon shall not give her light, and the stars shall fall from heaven, and the powers of the heavens shall be*

*shaken: And then shall appear the sign
of the Son of man in heaven: and then
shall all the tribes of the earth mourn,
and they shall see the Son of man coming in the clouds of heaven with power
and great glory (Matt. 24:29, 30).*

Further, Isaiah predicted that Babylon will
be destroyed as Sodom and Gomorrah were destroyed.

*<u>And Babylon,</u> the glory of king-
doms, the beauty of the Chaldees' ex-
cellency, <u>shall be as when God over-
threw Sodom and Gomorrah</u> (Isa.
13:19).*

Sodom and Gomorrah were destroyed by
fire and brimstone in a single night. Babylon has
never been destroyed in that manner. In the past
Babylon was taken in battle again and again, but
it was never suddenly destroyed. Instead, it fell
into decay over a period of centuries.

Isaiah's prophecy that Babylon will be suddenly destroyed is yet to be fulfilled. Verse 17 of
this chapter of The Revelation says that Babylon
will be destroyed in one hour. That sudden destruction of Babylon, when it occurs, will fulfill
Isaiah's prophecy.

Jeremiah also foretold the sudden destruction of Babylon. Like Isaiah, he predicted that

Babylon will fall suddenly, and like John in The Revelation he predicted that people will howl for her.

> _Babylon is suddenly fallen_ and destroyed: _howl for her;_ take balm for her pain, if so be she may be healed.
> We would have healed Babylon, but she is not healed: _forsake her, and let us go every one into his own country: for her judgment reacheth unto heaven,_ and is lifted up even to the skies (Jer. 51:8, 9).

In verse 19 of this chapter of The Revelation we are told that people will weep and wail over Babylon. That will fulfill the prediction of Jeremiah that people will _howl for her._

When Babylon is rebuilt, its location and the oil riches of the country will make it one of the commercial centers of the world. When it is destroyed, its destruction will cause great distress among the nations of the world.

The idea of rebuilding Babylon is not new. While Saddam Hussein was in power he planned to rebuild the city. He believed that he was descended from Nebuchadnezzar and was the heir to his throne. He worked at uncovering the ancient ruins of Babylon for several years before Desert Storm. Only Desert Storm and the Iraq War that started in 2003 kept him from rebuilding the city and reigning from there as Nebuchadnezzar had reigned in the glory of his kingdom.

Contents of Chapter 18

An Astounding Announcement

1 <u>And after these things</u> I saw another angel come down from heaven, having great power; and <u>the earth was lightened with his glory.</u>

2 And <u>he cried mightily </u>with a strong voice, saying, <u>Babylon the great is fallen, is fallen, </u>and is become the habitation of devils, and the hold of every foul spirit, and a cage of every unclean and hateful bird.

The astonishing announcement made in verse 2 is so important that a mighty angel came down from Heaven and made it in a strong voice. The power and glory of the angel and his strong voice underscores the importance of the message that *Babylon the great is fallen, is fallen.*

Babylon's Influence

3 For <u>all nations have drunk of the wine of the wrath of her fornication,</u> and <u>the kings of the earth have committed fornication with her,</u> and the merchants of the earth are waxed rich through the abundance of her delicacies.

Rebuilt Babylon will not only become a center of trade and commerce, it will be a center of false religion. Businesses of the world will be enriched by trading there, and the people of the world will be corrupted by its false religion.

A Warning to God's People

4 And <u>I heard another voice</u> from heaven, saying, <u>Come out of her, my people, that ye be not partakers of her sins,</u> and that ye receive not of her plagues.

Many people will go to Babylon to work and conduct business. Among them will be some of God's people. God will be concerned for them, and, as He warned Lot and his family to leave Sodom and Gomorrah before its destruction, He will warn them to *Come out of her.*

The End of God's Patience

5 For <u>her sins have reached unto heaven</u>, and God hath remembered her iniquities.

6 <u>Reward her</u> even as she rewarded you, and double unto <u>her double according to her works: in the cup which she hath filled fill to her double.</u>

7 How much <u>she hath glorified herself,</u> and lived deliciously, so much torment and sorrow give her: <u>for she saith in her heart, I sit a queen, and am no widow, and shall see no sorrow.</u>

Babylon's cup of sin will be twice full we are told in verse 6. She will be proud of her sinful practices and will boast that she will know no sorrow. God hates pride, and the sins of Babylon and her pride will not go unnoticed. The day of reckoning for the wicked city will come.

Destruction by Fire

8 <u>Therefore shall her plagues come in one day</u>, death, and mourning, and famine; and <u>she shall be utterly burned with fire:</u> for strong is the Lord God who judgeth her.

Verse 8 tells us that the city will be destroyed by fire in one day. That means that the destruction will be sudden.

The Lament of the Kings

9 *And the kings of the earth*, who have committed fornication and lived deliciously with her, *shall bewail her, and lament for her*, when they shall see the smoke of her burning.

10 *Standing afar off for the fear of her torment, saying, Alas, alas, that great city Babylon, that mighty city! for in one hour is thy judgment come.*

11 And *the merchants of the earth shall weep and mourn over her; for no man buyeth their merchandise any more:*

Verse 9 tells us that the kings of the earth will lament over the destruction of commercial Babylon. That is proof that ecclesiastical Babylon and commercial Babylon are not the same. The kings will rejoice when ecclesiastical Babylon is destroyed, but they will lament when commercial Babylon is destroyed.

It is likely that commercial Babylon will be destroyed by a nuclear bomb. Verse 10 tells of kings standing far away from the burning city for the fear of her torment. Verse 15 tells of merchants standing far from the city for fear, and verse 17 tells of sailors staying far from the city for the same reason. Fear of radiation from a nuclear bomb would cause men to stay away from the destroyed city.

The destruction of commercial Babylon will be a shock to the economy of the world. The stock markets of the world will crash, and banks will fail. World commerce will be at a standstill. Ships will be unable to deliver their cargo, and stores will close for lack of business. The merchants of the world will mourn because of business failures.

The valuable merchandise in the city will be destroyed, and radioactive fallout will contaminate goods in other parts of the country. For that reason there will be no market for anything that is left. The following verses give a list of the valuable merchandise that no one will buy.

The Spoiled Merchandise of Babylon

12 The merchandise of <u>gold</u>, and <u>silver</u>, and <u>precious stones</u>, and <u>of pearls</u>, and <u>fine linen</u>, and <u>purple</u>, and <u>silk</u>, and <u>scarlet</u>, and all <u>thyine wood</u>, and all manner <u>vessels of ivory</u>, and all manner <u>vessels of most precious wood</u>, and of <u>brass</u>, and <u>iron</u>, and <u>marble</u>,

13 And <u>cinnamon</u>, and <u>odours</u>, and <u>ointments</u>, and <u>frankincense</u>, and <u>wine</u>, and <u>oil</u>, and <u>fine flour</u>, and <u>wheat</u>, and <u>beasts</u>, and <u>sheep</u>, and <u>horses</u>, and *chariots, and slaves, and souls of men.*

14 And the fruits that thy soul lusted after are departed from thee, and all things which were dainty and goodly are departed from thee, and thou shalt find them no more at all.

Merchants Weeping Over the City

15 The merchants of these things, which were made rich by her, shall stand afar off for the fear of her torment, weeping and wailing.

Verse 15 repeats the information from verse 10 that merchants will stand far from the city for fear of its destruction. Only a nuclear bomb could cause such fear. The verse also speaks of weeping and wailing. There will be grief over both business losses and the loss of friends and family members.

The Lament of the Merchants

16 And saying, Alas, alas, that great city, that was clothed in fine linen, and purple, and scarlet, and decked with gold, and precious stones, and pearls!

17 For in one hour so great riches is come to nought. And every shipmaster, and all the company in ships, and sailors, and as many as trade by sea, stood afar off,

18 And cried when they saw the smoke of her burning, saying, <u>What city is like unto this great city!</u>

In verse 16 the merchants mourn over the loss of the great city, lamenting that it was *clothed in fine linen, and purple, and scarlet, and decked with gold, and precious stones, and pearls!*

In verses 17 they lament that, . . . *in one hour so great riches is come to nought.* In verse 18 they cry, *What city is like unto this great city!*

Doubtless the rebuilt city will be one of the finest cities in the world.

Sudden Destruction

19 And they cast dust on their heads, and cried, weeping and wailing, saying, Alas, alas, that great city, wherein were made rich all that had ships in the sea by reason of her costliness! for <u>in one hour is she made desolate.</u>

In verse 19 we are again told of the wealth of the city. *Alas, alas, that great city, wherein were made rich all that had ships in the sea by reason of her costliness!* We are told again in verse 19 that the city will be suddenly destroyed. *. . . for in one hour is she made desolate.*

Only an nuclear bomb or an act of God could destroy a large city so completely in a single hour.

Rejoicing in Heaven

20 <u>Rejoice over her, thou heaven,</u>
and ye holy apostles and prophets; for
God hath avenged you on her.

The destruction of Babylon will cause great sorrow on earth, but verse 20 tells us that, the holy apostles and prophets and the hosts of Heaven will rejoice over the destruction of the wicked city.

The destruction of Babylon will be the beginning of the end for the forces of evil. Satan, the Antichrist and the false prophet will soon be defeated in the Battle of Armageddon and cast into the lake of fire and brimstone.

A Symbol of Destruction

21 And <u>a mighty angel took up a</u>
<u>stone like a great millstone, and cast it</u>
<u>into the sea, saying, Thus with violence</u>
<u>shall that great city Babylon be thrown</u>
<u>down,</u> and shall be found no more at all.

In verse 21 we read of a mighty angel casting a stone that looks like a great millstone into the sea. From earlier chapters we know that the sea is a symbol of people. The angel casting the stone into the sea speaks of something with terrible destructive power being dropped upon the people of the city of Babylon.

The End of All Activity

22 And the voice of harpers, and musicians, and of pipers, and trumpeters, shall be heard no more at all in thee; and no craftsman, of whatsoever craft he be, shall be found any more in thee; and the sound of a millstone shall be heard no more at all in thee;

23 And the light of a candle shall shine no more at all in thee; and the voice of the bridegroom and of the bride shall be heard no more at all in thee: for thy merchants were the great men of the earth; for by thy sorceries were all nations deceived.

Babylon will be a dead city after its destruction. Verses 22 and 23 give us a picture of the end of all activity in the city. There will be no music, no craftsmen at work, no lights in the night, no merchants selling merchandise, and no people getting married.

The Epitaph of the City

24 And in her was found the blood of prophets, and of saints, and of all that were slain upon the earth.

In the last verse of the chapter the blood of martyred prophets and saints cries from the ashes of the fallen city.

Both false religion and godless government had their beginning in Babylon. That made it a city against God and for Satan. The city has long been in ruins, but its influence remains. It has corrupted the world with false religion. It has advanced the kingdom of Satan and martyred the saints of God. When Babylon is rebuilt it will not be different. It will still be a city in rebellion. For that reason there will be rejoicing in Heaven when it is destroyed.

Chapter 19

Introduction to Chapter 19

*T*he judgment of the two Babylons is past, and chapter 19 is like the rising of the sun after a dark night of unutterable storms. Instead of exclamations of grief, such as we had in chapter 18, this is a chapter of rejoicing. It contains four alleluias. The Hebrew form of alleluia is the well-known hallelujah. In any language hallelujah is praise to our God.

There is reason for the hallelujahs in this chapter. It begins with praise and ends with the Second Coming of Christ and the defeat of Antichrist and his armies.

In the last chapter the kings and merchants cried, *Alas* six times. In verse 10 the kings cried, *Alas, alas that great city Babylon, that mighty city! for in one hour is thy judgment come.* In verse 16 the merchants exclaim, *Alas, alas, that great city, . . .* And in verse 19, with weeping and wailing, the merchants say, *Alas, alas, that great city, . . .* There is no lamenting in chapter 19. It is the chapter of rejoicing.

Contents of Chapter 19

1. The four alleluias (verses 1-4)
2. The command to praise God (verse 5)
3. The praise of multitudes (verse 6)
4. The marriage of the Lamb (verses 7, 8)
5. The guest at the wedding (verse 9)
6. Angel worship forbidden (verse 10)
7. The glorious appearing of Christ (verses 11-13)
8. The King's army (verse 14)
9. The sword of victory (verse 15)
10. The King of all kings (verse 16)
11. Victory proclaimed (verses 17, 18)
12. Antichrist's army (verse 19)
13. The outcome of the battle (verses 20, 21)

The Four Alleluias

1 And after these things I heard a great voice of much people in heaven, saying, Alleluia; Salvation, and glory, and honour, and power, unto the Lord our God:

2 For true and righteous are his judgments: for he hath judged the great whore, which did corrupt the earth with her fornication, and hath avenged the blood of his servants at her hand.

3 And again they said, Alleluia. And her smoke rose up for ever and ever.

4 And the four and twenty elders and the four beasts fell down and wor-

shipped God that sat on the throne, saying, Amen; Alleluia.

The first alleluia in the chapter is found in verse 1. There many people are saying, *Alleluia; Salvation, and glory, and honour, and power, unto the Lord our God.*

The second alleluia is in verse 3. It is the alleluia of rejoicing because of the destruction of Babylon. *And again they said, Alleluia. And her smoke rose up for ever and ever.*

The third alleluia is found in verse 4. There we have the twenty-four elders, and the four seraphim worshiping God and saying, *Amen; Alleluia.*

The fourth alleluia is in verse 6. There John heard a great multitude saying, as the voice of many waters, and as the voice of mighty thunderings, *Alleluia: for the Lord God omnipotent reigneth.*

There is reason for the alleluias, Both ecclesiastical Babylon and commercial Babylon have been destroyed, and that is the beginning of the end of Antichrist's reign.

It is important to see who is rejoicing. The twenty-four elders, symbolizing the church, are rejoicing, and the seraphim, the highest order of angels, are worshiping and praising God. The elders and the seraphim often appear together in The Revelation, and usually they are praising God.

The Command to Praise God

5 And <u>a voice came out of the throne, saying, Praise our God, all ye his servants,</u> and ye that fear him, both small and great.

The voice that came from the throne in verse 5 is not identified, and commentators are not sure who gave the order to praise God. It cannot be the voice of God, for the voice said, *Praise our God, all ye his servants.* The speaker was evidently also a servant of God, for he said, *Praise our God.* That is as much as we know about the voice from the throne.

The Praise of Multitudes

6 And I heard as it were <u>the voice of a great multitude, and as the voice of many waters, and as the voice of mighty thunderings, saying, Alleluia: for the Lord God omnipotent reigneth.</u>

Verse 6 tells of a great multitude praising God. The saved of all ages will comprise a mighty company. All the people of Old Testament times who trusted in the Lamb of God, foreshadowed by every lamb that was offered upon an altar, will be in Heaven. All who have received Jesus as their Saviour since He died on Calvary will be in Heaven, and all the children who have died before the age of accountability will be there. What a day it will be when the alleluias of this mighty throng rise before the throne of God and echo His praises throughout the universe.

The Marriage of the Lamb

7 Let us <u>be glad and rejoice, and give honour to him: for the marriage of the Lamb is come, and his wife hath made herself ready.</u>

8 And to her was granted that she should be arrayed in fine linen, clean and white: for the fine linen is the righteousness of saints.

Verse 7 tells us, *The Marriage of the Lamb is come!* That will be another reason for rejoicing. While Jesus was on earth He told His disciples that after He returned to Heaven, He would come back to receive them unto Himself (John 14:3). He will keep that promise and receive them in the rapture,

As Isaac went forth to meet Rebekah when the servant was bringing her from a far country to be his bride (Gen. 24:63), the Son of God will come forth to meet His bride in the air when she rises to meet Him from the far country of the world.

What a blessed event that will be! Time is waiting for that hour. The Old Testament saints of God are waiting for that hour. The ransomed church is waiting for that hour. Angels and archangels are waiting for that hour, and the Son of God is waiting for that hour.

The Guests at the Wedding

9 And *he saith unto me, Write, Blessed are they which are called unto the marriage supper of the Lamb. And he saith unto me, These are the true sayings of God.*

An angel who told John to write about the invited guests at the marriage supper. That will probably be the same angel that talked to him in Revelation 17:1.

There has been much controversy regarding the identity of the guests at the wedding. The guests cannot be the church, for the church will be the bride. The guests will not be the angels. They will only be spectators. There are two companies of saved people who are not in the church. They are those who were saved before there was a church and those who will be saved after the church is taken out of the world at the rapture. It is logical to believe that these two companies will be the guests at the wedding. What a glorious company of guests they will be.

Angel Worship Forbidden

10 And *I fell at his feet to worship him. And he said unto me, See thou do it not: I am thy fellow-servant, and of thy brethren that have the testimony of*

Jesus: worship God: for the testimony of Jesus is the spirit of prophecy.

In verse 10 John fell at the feet of the angel that told him of the marriage of the Lamb. That was an act of worship, but the angel forbade him, saying *See thou do it not.* Then he reminded John that they were both servants of God.

Satan and his angels are the only angels that desire to be worshiped, and they are fallen angels. Those who worship Satan or his angels are joining in rebellion against God, and that is the worst kind of idolatry.

The Glorious Appearing of Christ

11 And <u>I saw heaven opened, and behold a white horse; and he that sat upon him was called Faithful and True,</u> and in righteousness he doth judge and make war.

12 His eyes were as a flame of fire, and <u>on his head were many crowns;</u> and he had a name written, that no man knew, but he himself.

13 And he was clothed with a vesture dipped in blood: and his name is called <u>The Word of God.</u>

In verse 11 we come to the second division of the chapter. Heaven is open, and our Saviour appears riding on a white horse. Conquering generals in the past often rode upon white horses. It will be fitting for the King of kings to ride upon a white horse in His glorious Second Coming.

Doubtless the white horse is a symbol of some means of travel through space. Means of travel in space is not unheard of in the Bible. The Bible says that God rode upon a cherub (2 Sam. 22:11 and Psa. 18:10). In 2 Kings 2:11 we read that Elijah went to Heaven in a chariot of fire.

Verse 14 tells us that the armies that will follow our Lord will also ride upon white horses. While heavenly chariots and heavenly horses are symbolic, they indicate that our Lord and His mighty army will have means of travel through space that is beyond anything that has been or will ever be developed in this world.

Jesus will be wearing many crowns when He comes to earth again, and He will rule all the kingdoms of the world. In Revelation 5:5 Jesus was found worthy to break the seals on the book containing the title deed of the earth. Now the time has come for Him to take possession of the earth and reign over it.

Verse 13 says that Jesus is wearing a vesture dipped in blood, and that his name is called, *The Word of God.* The vesture dipped in blood is a symbol of His death on the cross, and being called the Word of God speaks of His deity.

Jesus is only called *The Word of God* in the

New Testament writings of John. That is one of the evidences that John was the author of The Revelation.

The King's Army

14 And the <u>armies which were in heaven</u> followed him upon white horses, <u>clothed in fine linen, white and clean.</u>

The church will compose much of the vast army of the Lord. In Jude 14 we read, *Behold the Lord cometh with ten thousands* (myriads) *of his saints.* Old Testaments saints will also accompany the Lord at His Second Coming. In Zechariah 14:5b we read, *And the Lord my God shall come, <u>and all the saints with thee.</u>*

Angels will also be in the Lord's army. Paul wrote concerning them . . . *when the Lord Jesus shall be revealed from heaven <u>with his mighty angels,</u> In flaming fire taking vengeance on them that know not God, and that obey not the gospel of our Lord Jesus Christ (2 Thess. 1:7, 8).*

The Sword of Victory

15 <u>And out of his mouth goeth a sharp sword, that with it he should smite the nations:</u> and he shall rule them with a rod of iron: <u>and he treadeth the winepress of the fierceness and wrath of Almighty God.</u>

The sword going out of the mouth of the Son

of God suggests that He will smite wicked nations with the same power that God used when he spoke the worlds into existence. The prophet Isaiah wrote of God punishing the wicked with the breath of His lips.

> *... and he shall smite the earth with the rod of his mouth, and with the breath of his lips shall he slay the wicked (Isa. 11:4b).*

Verse 15 speaks of the wrath of God. The Second Coming of Christ will be a time of judgment upon a wicked world that has rebelled against God.

The King of All Kings

> *16 And he hath on his vesture and on his thigh a name written, <u>KING OF KINGS, AND LORD OF LORDS.</u>*

Jesus will come as King of kings, and Lord of lords. He was born in a lowly manger, but God has given Him a name above every name (Phil. 2:9). He has all power in Heaven and on earth (Matt. 28:18). In His Second Coming He will come as *KING OF KINGS, AND LORD OF LORDS,* and He will defeat Satan and take control of the world.

Victory Proclaimed

> *17 <u>And I saw an angel standing in the sun; and he cried with a loud voice,</u>*

saying to all the fowls that fly in the midst of heaven, Come and gather your-selves together unto the supper of the great God;

18 That ye may eat the flesh of kings, and the flesh of captains, and the flesh of mighty men, and the flesh of horses, and of them that sit on them, and the flesh of all men, both free and bond, both small and great.

The angel standing in the sun (verse 17) will proclaim victory before the battle is fought. In his characteristic way Satan will believe that he can win the Battle of Armageddon, but his doom will be sealed before the battle starts. God is al-mighty. Satan's power is limited, and he and his puppet kings and all their armies will be de-stroyed.

Antichrist's Army

19 And I saw the beast, and the kings of the earth, and their armies, gathered together to make war against him that sat on the horse, and against his army.

Antichrist will see Christ and His mighty army coming from Heaven before they reach the earth. He will know that Jesus is returning to Jerusalem, and he will assemble his army and the armies of his puppet kings and bring them to the valley of Esdraelon, under the shadow of Megiddo, for the battle.

The Outcome of the Battle

20 And <u>the beast was taken, and with him the false prophet</u> that wrought miracles before him, with which he deceived them that had received the mark of the beast, and them that worshipped his image. <u>These both were cast alive into a lake of fire burning with brimstone.</u>

21 And <u>the remnant were slain with the sword of him that sat upon the horse</u>, which sword proceeded out of his mouth: and all the fowls were filled with their flesh.

The details of the Battle of Armageddon are not given. Evidently it will be a short battle. There will be no casualties in the Lord's army, but only a remnant of the armies of Antichrist will be alive when the battle is over. The remnant that remains will be slain with the sword of the Lord's mouth.

Antichrist and the false prophet will be captured and cast alive into a lake of fire and brimstone. A thousand years later, when Satan is cast into the lake of fire, they will still be there, for hell is eternal.

There is no such place as purgatory where

the wicked will go temporarily. Purgatory is not mentioned in the Bible. All who go to hell will remain there forever. Heaven is also eternal. Those who go there will enjoy unending ages of health, happiness, and the service for the Lord.

> *Therefore are <u>they before the throne of God, and serve him day and night in his temple: and he that sitteth on the throne shall dwell among them.</u>*
>
> <u>*They shall hunger no more, neither thirst any more; neither shall the sun light on them, nor any heat.*</u>
>
> <u>*For the Lamb which is in the midst of the throne shall feed them, and shall lead them unto living fountains of waters: and God shall wipe away all tears from their eyes*</u> *(Rev. 7:15-17).*

In the 23rd Psalm the Lord is pictured as the shepherd who leads His sheep to green pastures and beside still water. After the Lord's Second Coming He will still be the shepherd of His people. He will feed them and lead them beside fountains of living waters. God will wipe away all tears from their eyes, and there will be no more tears forever. Let all the people of God say, *Alleluia.*

Chapter 20

Introduction to Chapter 20

We now come to the study of the fifth and final section of The Revelation. This section is covered in the last three chapters of the book. It is about events that will occur after the end of the tribulation and the Second Coming of Christ.

Chapter 20 deals with end-time events that are not covered in earlier chapters. Chapters 21 and 22 contain John's visions of the new Heaven and the new earth, and they give us a view of Heaven not found elsewhere in the Bible.

Chapter 20 is a most important chapter. It is like an open window that gives us a view of some outstanding events that will take place after the Second Coming of Christ.

This chapter can best be understood when studied under four divisions as follows.
Division # 1, The Incarceration of Satan
Division # 2, The Millennial Reign of Christ

Division #3, Satan Released From Prison
Division #4, The White Throne Judgment

Contents of Chapter 20

Division #1, The Incarceration of Satan

  1. The Arresting Angel (verses 1, 2)
  2. The Bottomless Pit (verse 3)

Division #2, The Millennial Reign of Christ

  1. Reigning With Christ (verse 4)
  2. The First Resurrection (verses 5, 6)

Division #3, Satan Released From Prison

  1. Man's final test (verse 7)
  2. Satan's last war (verse 8)
  3. Satan defeated (verse 9)
  4. Satan's final punishment (verse 10)

Division #4, The White Throne Judgment

  1. The awesome throne of God (verse 11)
  2. The judgment of the wicked dead (verse 12)
  3. The resurrection of the wicked dead (verse 13)
  4. The second death (verses 14, 15)

The Incarceration of Satan
The Arresting Angel

1 And I saw an angel come down from heaven, <u>having the key of the bottomless pit and a great chain in his hand.</u>

2 And he laid hold on <u>the dragon, that old serpent, which is the Devil, and Satan, and bound him a thousand years,</u>

Verses 1 and 2 tell us that a mighty angel will come down from Heaven with a great chain in his hand and the key to the bottomless pit. He will have the power and the authority to arrest Satan and bind him for a thousand years. In chapter 9 a fallen angel was given the key to the bottomless pit. He was Satan's angel, and he could only do what he was allowed to do. This angel from Heaven already has the key.

Some skeptics have objected that an angel would not use an iron chain to bind the devil. The Bible does not say that the angel had an iron chain. It only says that the angel had a great chain in his hand.

God has chains that are not made of any kind of metal. For instance, He has bound the earth to the sun and the moon to the earth with invisible chains that no man can break. The chain in this verse is symbolic of something God uses to confine fallen angels. In 2 Peter 2:4 and Jude 6 we read of angels that are bound in everlasting chains of darkness.

There is no mistaking the identity of Satan in this passage. Verse two calls him, . . . *the dragon, that old serpent, which is the Devil, and Satan.*

The thousand years that Satan will be bound is not to be spiritualized. It will be a literal period of a thousand years. We do not spiritualize reference to the length of the tribulation. We believe that it will last seven years, and that the last half will last 42 months (Rev. 11:2), or 1260 days (Rev. 11:3). Just so, a thousand years means a thousand years. The thousand years is mentioned six times in this chapter, and there is no reason to believe that it does not mean a literal thousand years.

The Bottomless Pit

3 And cast him into the <u>bottomless pit,</u> and shut him up, and set a seal upon him, that he should deceive the nations no more, <u>till the thousand years should be fulfilled:</u> and after that <u>he must be loosed a little season.</u>

The angel will cast Satan into the bottomless pit. The bottomless pit is not the same as the lake of fire. The Greek word, "abussos," translated bottomless pit, is the abyss where fallen angels and demon spirits are imprisoned.

Revelation 9:1-3 tells us that when the fallen angel opened the bottomless pit, smoke and locust-like demon spirits came out and tormented men for five months. In verse 11 of that chapter we read that the locusts had a king over them. In the Hebrew tongue their king is called Abaddon, and in the Greek tongue he is called Apollyon.

And <u>they had a king over them, which is the angel of the bottomless pit, whose name in the Hebrew tongue is Abaddon, but in the Greek tongue hath</u>

his name Apollyon (Rev. 9:11).

Satan will spend a thousand years in the bottomless pit. In verse 7 we are told that after a thousand years Satan will be loosed out of his prison for a little season. Then in verse 10 we read that he will be cast into the lake of fire and brimstone, the place of eternal punishment.

The Millennial Reign of Christ
Reigning With Christ

4 And I saw thrones, and they sat upon them, and judgment was given unto them: and I saw the souls of them that were beheaded for the witness of Jesus, and for the word of God, and which had not worshipped the beast, neither his image, neither had received his mark upon their foreheads, or in their hands; and they lived and reigned with Christ a thousand years.

In verse 4 John saw the enthroned church and the martyrs from the tribulation reigning with Christ, and he was told that they reigned with Christ for a thousand years. The thousand year reign of Christ is called the millennium. Some object that the word millennium because it is not found in the Bible. That does not mean that the word should not be used. The word millennium is from the Latin words "Mille" and "Annum," meaning a 1000 years. We use millennium to mean a 1000 years just as we use century to mean

100 years.

The First Resurrection

5 <u>But the rest of the dead</u> lived not again until the thousand years were finished. <u>This is the first resurrection.</u>

6 <u>Blessed and holy is he that hath part in the first resurrection:</u> on such the second death hath no power, but <u>they shall be priests of God and of Christ, and shall reign with him a thousand years.</u>

The first resurrection will be the resurrection of the dead in Christ. They will rise when Christ comes to rapture the church. The Apostle Paul has given a description of the coming of the Lord and the first resurrection.

For the Lord himself shall descend from heaven with a shout, with the voice of the archangel, and with the trump of God: and <u>the dead in Christ shall rise first</u> (1 Thess. 4:16).

Those who will be in the first resurrection are called blessed, for they will be priests of God and of Christ, and they will reign with Him for a thousand years. The wicked dead will not rise until after the thousand year reign of Christ and the church.

Satan Released From Prison
Man's Final Test

7 And when the thousand years are expired, Satan shall be loosed out of his prison,

There has been much conjecture about why Satan will be loosed from prison before he is sentenced to the lake of fire. It is almost as if he will be in jail for a thousand years and then will be released on bond, but that cannot be, for no bond will be posted. There has to be another reason for Satan being released.

Some writers have suggested that Satan will be loosed to show that man is a failure, even when there has been no tempter on earth for a thousand years. That may well be the reason.

God has tested man in every dispensation in the past. (A dispensation is a period of time during which man is tested with respect to obedience to the revealed will of God at that time).

Scofield lists seven dispensations in the Scofield Bible as follows: (1) the dispensation of Innocence, (2) the dispensation of Conscience, (3) the dispensation of Human Government, (4) the dispensation of Promise, (5) the dispensation of Law, (6) the dispensation of Grace, and (7) the dispensation of the Kingdom.

The first five dispensations have passed, and we are now living in the sixth. Man has failed every test in all the past dispensations, and he is a dismal failure in the present dispensation. During the millennium kingdom, man will fail again. There will be many sinful, rebellious people living on earth during the millennium reign of Christ. That is why He will rule with a rod of iron (Rev. 19:15). When Satan is released from prison, sinful people will be ready to join him in a war against the Son of God.

Satan's Last War

8 And shall go out to deceive the nations which are in the four quarters of the earth, Gog and Magog, <u>to gather them together to battle: the number of whom is as the sand of the sea.</u>

After Satan is released he will gather an army of rebellious men and make a last desperate effort to defeat Jesus and take back the kingdoms of the world. The fact that many will follow Satan in that war will demonstrate that man is a failure even when Satan is bound and Christ is on the throne. The only hope for fallen man is repentance and faith in the Lord Jesus Christ, and multitudes will refuse to trust Him even when they see Him on His throne.

Satan Defeated

9 And they went up on the breadth of the earth, and compassed the camp of the saints about, and the beloved city: and fire came down from God out of heaven, and devoured them.

Satan's last war will be short and decisive, for God will intervene, and fire will come down from Heaven and devour his army of men. Satan will not be destroyed by the fire because he is a spirit, and fire will not destroy a spirit.

Satan's Final Punishment

10 And the devil that deceived them was cast into the lake of fire and brimstone, where the beast and the false prophet are, and shall be tormented day and night for ever and ever.

Satan has been a deceiver from the time of his fall. When he fell he deceived one third of the angels, and they joined him in his rebellion. He deceived Eve in the garden of Eden, and she sinned and led her husband to sin. Satan has been deceiving mankind ever since. His last army of men will be deceived into believing that they can win the war against the King of kings. The deceiver will fail and will be cast into the lake of fire with the beast and the false prophet.

The White Throne Judgment
The Awesome Throne of God

11 And I saw a great white throne,

and him that sat on it, from whose face
the earth and the heaven fled away; and
there was found no place for them.

God is so powerful and so glorious that even
the heavens flee from His presence. Moses once
asked God to let him see His Glory. God's reply
was, *Thou canst not see my face: for there shall
no man see me, and live (Ex. 33:20).* Only after
we reach the spirit world will we be able to see
God (Job. 19:26; Matt. 5:8). It is not possible to
imagine the fear the wicked dead will feel when
they stand before God to be judged.

The Judgment of the Wicked Dead

12 And I saw the dead, small and
great, stand before God; and the books
were opened: and another book was
opened, which is the book of life: and
the dead were judged out of those things
which were written in the books, accord-
ing to their works.

When the wicked dead stand before God to
be judged some books will be opened. It is not
possible to know what God's books are like, but
the Bible makes it clear that God has some de-
tailed record books. He even has a record of
where we were born. In Psalm 87:6 we read,

The Lord shall count, when he

writeth up the people, that this man was born there. Selah.

Not only is the birthplace of every person known, even the hairs on their heads are numbered (Matt. 10:30).

One of God's books is the book of life (verse 15). Only the names of the saved are recorded there. Those whose names are not written in the book of life will be judged at the great white throne judgment. They are the wicked dead that we read about in the next verse.

The Resurrection of the Wicked Dead

13 And the sea gave up the dead which were in it; and death and hell delivered up the dead which were in them: and they were judged every man according to their works.

The Second Death

14 And death and hell were cast into the lake of fire. This is the second death.

15 And whosoever was not found written in the book of life was cast into the lake of fire.

In verses 13 and 14 we have a description of the resurrection of the wicked dead. Bodies will be raised from the sea, *the sea gave up the dead which were in it.* Dead bodies will come from their graves, and hell (Hades) will give up the spirits of the wicked that are in it. The Bible says, *and death and hell delivered up the dead which were in them.*

Not one saved person will be in that resurrection. It will be the resurrection of the wicked dead. God knows where all the dead are buried, whether on land or in the sea.

The saved will not be judged with the lost. They will be judged at the judgment seat of Christ. That will be an entirely different judgment. The time will be different, the place will be different, and the results will be different. At the judgment seat of Christ the righteous will be judged and rewarded according to the works they have done as children of God (2 Cor. 5:10).

Verse 12 of this chapter of The Revelation tells us the lost will be judged according to what is written in God's record book. Verse 13 tells us that they will be judged according to their works, but their works are works of iniquity. Lost people will have nothing to offer God but their works, and Paul makes it clear that no one can be saved by their works.

> *Knowing that a man is not justified by the works of the law, but by the faith of Jesus Christ . . . (Gal. 2:16).*

A final search of the Book of Life will be

made, and those whose names are not written there will be sent to hell. No one on earth, or in Heaven, or in hell will be able to say that justice has not been done.

Names written in other places will not suffice. A name in the hall of fame will not get one into Heaven. A name on the deeds to great properties will not get one into Heaven. A name on an ornate tomb or monument will not get one into Heaven. There will be no reprieve and no second chance. All who have rejected the Saviour will suffer for their rejection and their sins.

Not one person in this judgment will be saved. Verse 15 tells us that death and hell were cast into the lake of fire. That means that dead bodies and lost souls will be cast into the lake of fire, and that is the second death. The first death is the death of the body. The second death is the never ending, worse-than-death, eternal suffering of the lost in the lake of fire.

To end up in hell will be a terrible fate, but there must be a place of incarceration for the devil and his angels, and for people who have served him. If people could go to Heaven with their sinful natures, they would be miserable. They do not enjoy being with saved people on earth, and they would not enjoy being with them in Heaven. If the lost could go to Heaven, pride, envy, covetousness, and jealousy would make them bad neighbors. They would lose their tempers, hold grudges, and hate others. They would lie, gossip, cheat, steal, and do other wicked things, just as they did on earth.

In this world there are people who must be imprisoned for the protection of others. The same will be true in eternity. For that reason God will not allow anyone with a sinful nature to enter Heaven. There has to be a place where the devil and his angels and unsaved people will spend eternity, and the Bible calls that place hell.

It is well that the Book of Revelation does not end with the description of the judgment of the wicked and their terrible fate. That would be a terrible way for the Book to end.

The next two chapters will take us into the glory world, and we will share the wonderful visions that John had of the things God has prepared for the redeemed. That will be a fitting climax to the conflict of the ages.

Chapter 21

Introduction to Chapter 21

*I*n this chapter John was given a vision of the new Heaven and the new earth, but he was not told when they were created. Many believe that the new earth will not be created until after the millennial reign of Christ, but that is not Scriptural, nor is it logical.

John was not the only one to write about the new Heaven and the new earth. There are three other references to the new Heaven and the new earth in the Bible. They are in Isaiah 65:17, 18; Isaiah 66:22, and 2 Peter 3:13. These references show that the new Heaven and the new earth will be created before the millennial reign of Christ.

Almost 700 years before the birth of Christ, Isaiah wrote, *For, behold, I create new heavens and a new earth . . . (Isa. 65:17).*

In the rest of the chapter Isaiah describes conditions as they will be on earth during the millennial reign of Christ. The passage from

Isaiah follows.

> *17 For, behold, I create new heav-*
> *ens and a new earth: and the former*
> *shall not be remembered, nor come into*
> *mind.*
>
> *20 <u>There shall be no more thence*
> *an infant of days, nor an old man that*
> *hath not filled his days: for the child*
> *shall die an hundred years old; but the*
> *sinner being an hundred years old</u> shall*
> *be accursed.*
>
> *22 <u>They shall not build, and another*
> *inhabit; they shall not plant, and an-*
> *other eat: for as the days of a tree are*
> *the days of my people, and mine elect*
> *shall long enjoy the work of their hands.</u>*
>
> *23 <u>They shall not labor in vain, nor*
> *bring forth for trouble</u> . . .*
>
> *25 <u>The wolf and the lamb shall feed*
> *together, and the lion shall eat straw like*
> *the bullock: and dust shall be the*
> *serpent's meat. They shall not hurt nor*
> *destroy in all my holy mountain, saith*
> *the LORD.</u>*

Isaiah's prophecy clearly shows that the new Heaven and the new earth will be created before the millennial reign of Christ begins. The curse of sin is upon the present earth. There will be no curse upon the new earth.

During the reign of Christ there will be peace and prosperity. Isaiah tells us that people will build houses and live in them and plant vineyards and eat the fruit of them. In Isaiah 65:23 we read that they will not labor in vain nor bring forth for trouble. That is a clear promise that God will not destroy what will be built during the thousand year reign of Christ.

Christ will come before the millennium, and at the time of His coming there will be every reason to destroy the world that wicked men have corrupted. The present world is filled with wicked music, narcotics, liquor, pornography, strip-joints, brothels, gambling, crime, wicked devices too numerous to mention, and weapons of war. All that will need to be destroyed before the reign of Christ begins. Peter, writing about the Second Coming of Christ, gives a graphic description of the day of the Lord and clearly says that the works of men will be burned up when He comes.

> *But the day of the Lord will come as a thief in the night; in the which the heavens shall pass away with a great noise, and the elements shall melt with fervent heat, the earth also and the works that are therein shall be burned up (2 Peter 3:10).*

Paul predicted the same event and tells us that Jesus will come in flaming fire, taking vengeance on them that know not God

> *. . . Jesus shall be revealed from heaven with his mighty angels. <u>In flaming fire taking vengeance on them that know not God</u> . . . (2 Thess. 1:7, 8).*

Isaiah also prophesied that the Lord will come with flaming fire and that much of the population of the earth will be destroyed.

> *For, <u>behold, the LORD will come with fire,</u> and with his chariots like a whirlwind, to render his anger <u>with fury, and his rebuke with flames of fire. . . . and the slain of the LORD shall be many</u> (Isa. 66:15-16).*

The burning of the earth will be the most catastrophic event ever to strike the planet, but, terrible as it will be, not all the people on earth will perish. John describes how some will survive by hiding in the dens and the rocks of the mountains.

> *And the kings of the earth, and the great men, and the rich men, and the chief captains, and the mighty men, and every bondman, and every free man, hid themselves in the dens and in the rocks of*

*the mountains; And said to the mountains
and rocks, Fall on us, and hide us from
the face of him that sitteth on the throne,
and from the wrath of the Lamb: For the
great day of his wrath is come; and who
shall be able to stand? (Rev. 6:15-17).*

Malachi brings out some interesting points regarding the burning of the earth.

*FOR, behold, the day cometh, that
shall burn as an oven; and all the proud,
yea, and all that do wickedly, shall be
stubble:* <u>*and the day that cometh shall*</u>
<u>*burn them up, saith the LORD of hosts,*</u>
*that it shall leave them neither root nor
branch.* <u>*But unto you that fear my name*</u>
<u>*shall the Sun of righteousness arise with*</u>
<u>*healing in his wings; and ye shall go*</u>
<u>*forth, and grow up as calves of the stall.*</u>
And ye shall tread down the wicked; <u>*for*</u>
<u>*they shall be ashes under the soles of*</u>
<u>*your feet*</u> *in the day that I shall do this,
saith the LORD of hosts. (Mal. 4:1-3).*

Malachi tells us that:

(1) The wicked will be burned.

(2) The Sun of righteousness will come with healing.

(3) The Jews will grow up like calves of the

stall.

(4) Survivors will tread the ashes of the wicked under their feet. That shows that the righteous will occupy this earth after the burning of the wicked. The figure of calves in the stall speaks of the care Israel will receive during the millennium.

The Earth Will Be Renewed

The present earth will not be annihilated. It will be renovated. Note what Peter wrote concerning the world that then was and the world that now is.

> *Whereby the world that then was, being overflowed with water, perished: But the heavens and the earth, which are now, by the same word are kept in store, reserved unto fire against the day of judgment and perdition of ungodly men (2 Pet. 3:6, 7).*

When the world was destroyed by water it did not cease to exist. The same will be true when the world is destroyed by fire. It will be renewed and will abide forever. The fact that the earth will never cease to exist is clearly predicted in several passages in the Bible. One example follows.

> *One generation passeth away, and another generation cometh: but the*

earth abideth forever (Ecc. 1:4).

There will be no wars and no diseases during the thousand year reign of Christ, and people will live for hundreds of years as they did before the flood. Concerning this Isaiah wrote:

> *There shall be no more thence an infant of days, nor an old man that hath not filled his days: for the child shall die an hundred years old . . . (Isa. 65:20).*

For these reasons there will be a population explosion. Israel will become a great nation, and the other nations of the earth will multiply greatly. Billions of people will be living on earth by the end of the millennium.

Contents of Chapter 21

1. The dawn of eternity (verses 1, 2)
2. The tabernacle of God (verse 3)
3. The end of tears (verse 4)
4. All things made new (verse 5)
5. Salvation full and free (verse 6)
6. Victory for overcomers (verses 7, 8)
7. The beginning of eternity (verse 9)
8. The vision fulfilled (verses 10, 11)
9. The gates of the city (verses 12, 13)
10. The foundations of the city (verse 14)
11. The measure of the city (verses 15, 16)
12. The measure of the wall (verse 17)
13. The city of gold (verse 18)
14. The beauty of the wall (verses 19, 20)

15. The gates of pearl (verse 21)
16. God is the temple (verse 22)
17. The light of the city (verse 23)
18. The saved nations (verses 24-27)

The Dawn of Eternity

1 And I saw a new heaven and a new earth: for the first heaven and the first earth were passed away; and there was no more sea.

2 And I John saw the holy city, new Jerusalem, coming down from God out of heaven, prepared as a bride adorned for her husband.

John had two visions in the first two verses of this chapter. In verse 1 he saw a new Heaven and a new earth. In verse 2 he saw the holy city, new Jerusalem, coming down from God out of Heaven, adorned as a bride is adorned for her husband.

As we saw in chapter 19, the last battle of earth has been fought, and Satan has been cast into the lake of fire. We are now ready for the new Heaven and the new earth.

John does not give a description of the new Jerusalem in verse 2. He only says that he saw it coming down from God out of Heaven. It is not until verse 10 that he begins to describe the city. It is not out of character for John to say that he saw the new Jerusalem coming out of Heaven without giving a description of what it looked like until later. That is a practice he follows throughout the book.

The Tabernacle of God

3 And I heard a great voice out of heaven saying, <u>Behold, the tabernacle of God is with men, and he will dwell with them, and they shall be his people, and God himself shall be with them, and be their God.</u>

A voice from Heaven told John that the tabernacle of God will be with men, and that He will dwell with them.

Almost fifteen hundred years before the birth of Christ, God told Moses to construct a tabernacle in the wilderness and to place the ark of the covenant in it. God promised that He would then come down and commune with him above the mercy seat (Ex. 25:22).

During the millennium God will again come down and dwell with His people (Ezek. 37:27). God's presence was important to Israel in the wilderness. It will be even more important to the Jewish people during the millennium.

The End of Tears

4 <u>And God shall wipe away all tears from their eyes;</u> and there shall be no more death, neither sorrow, nor cry-

ing, neither shall there be any more pain: for the former things are passed away.

This is the second time in The Revelation that God promises to wipe away all tears. In chapter 7, verse 14, He promised to wipe away the tears of tribulation saints. In this chapter He promised to wipe away all tears when He comes to dwell among men on earth.

All Things Made New

5 And he that sat upon the throne said, <u>Behold, I make all things new.</u> And he said unto me, Write: for these words are true and faithful.

In verse 5 John wrote about the preparation of the earth for the millennium. In verse 6 he wrote about salvation for all who thirst, and in verses 7 and 8 he shows the difference in overcomers (believers) and the fearful (unbelievers). It is not until verse 9 that he begins to write about the Lamb's wife and the city she will occupy during eternity.

Salvation Full and Free

6 And he said unto me, It is done. <u>I am Alpha and Omega,</u> the beginning and the end. <u>I will give unto him that is athirst of the fountain of the water of life freely.</u>

In verse 6 Jesus reminds us that He is the eternal Alpha and Omega, and that He will give the water of life freely to all who are thirsty. As we saw in the last chapter, there will be unsaved people on earth during the millennium. Jesus is offering them the water of life.

Victory for Overcomers

7 <u>He that overcometh </u>shall inherit all things; and <u>I will be his God, and he shall be my son.</u>

8 <u>But the fearful, and unbelieving,</u> and the abominable, and murderers, and whoremongers, and sorcerers, and idolaters, and all liars, <u>shall have their part in the lake which burneth with fire and brimstone: which is the second death.</u>

In verse 7 God speaks of overcomers and promises that they will inherit all things. In contrast, in verse 8, He speaks of the fearful and unbelieving. A list of the vilest sinners follows. There will be unbelievers on earth during the millennium, and they will be just as lost as the worst of sinners, and that they will go to hell just as the vilest sinners will.

The Beginning of Eternity

9 And there came unto me one of the seven angels which had the seven vials full of the seven last plagues, and talked with me, saying, Come hither, I will shew thee the bride, the Lamb's wife.

We come now to the beginning of eternity. In verse 2 John saw the new Jerusalem coming down from God out of Heaven, prepared as a bride adorned for her husband. In verse 9 the city is called the bride, the Lamb's wife. The wedding and the marriage supper of the Lamb are past. The church is now the Lamb's wife, and the city John saw will be her eternal home.

The Vision Fulfilled

10 And he carried me away in the spirit to a great and high mountain, and shewed me that great city, the holy Jerusalem, descending out of heaven from God,

11 Having the glory of God: and her light was like unto a stone most precious, even like a jasper stone, clear as crystal;

In verses 10 and 11 we learn four things about the city John saw.

1. The city was a great city.

2. It was the holy Jerusalem.

3. It was filled with the glory of God.

4. The light of the city made it look like a

huge, crystal jasper (diamond).

Verse 11 does not say that the city is a jasper. It says that the light of the city is like unto a jasper. That light was the glory of God shining from the city.

The Gates of the City

12 And had a wall great and high, <u>and had twelve gates,</u> and <u>at the gates twelve angels,</u> and names written thereon, which are the names of the twelve tribes of the children of Israel:

13 On the east three gates; on the north three gates; on the south three gates; and on the west three gates.

One of the most prominent features of the city will be its twelve gates of pearl. There are six interesting things about the gates.

1. The gates will be twelve in number.

2. The names of the twelve tribes of Israel are written on the gates.

We will not be able to enter the city without being reminded that we are indebted to Israel for our salvation. From Israel we got our Bible. From Israel we got our Saviour, and from Israel we got our church. The Bible tells us that we are built upon the foundation of the apostles and prophets (Eph. 2:20). The apostles and prophets were all Jews.

3. There were three gates on every side of the city. Three is the number of the Trinity. Those who enter the city from any point of the compass will be reminded of the three persons of the Trinity, God, the Father, Jesus, the Son, and the Holy Spirit.

4. The gates of the city are not there for protection. They are always open.

5. There will be an angel at every gate. The angels will not be there as celestial policemen to see that everyone who enters is worthy or has the correct credentials. Instead, they will be there to welcome home the children of God.

6. The gates are made of pearl. The meaning of the gates of pearl will be discussed after verse 21.

The Foundations of the City

14 And the wall of the city had twelve foundations, and in them the names of the twelve apostles of the Lamb.

The city has twelve foundations. It is not likely that the twelve foundations of the wall are built on top of each other. It is more likely that they are located between each of the twelve gates. However that may be, the twelve foundations will contain the names of the twelve apostles.

The Measure of the City

15 And <u>he that talked with me had a golden reed to measure the city, and the gates thereof, and the wall thereof.</u>

16 And <u>the city lieth foursquare</u>, and the length is as large as the breadth: and he measured the city with the reed, <u>twelve thousand furlongs. The length and the breadth and the height of it are equal.</u>

The city John saw was a cube. That speaks of the perfection of the city. A cube is the only object that cannot be improved. Change any dimension of a cube, and it is no longer a cube. The city will be perfect, there will be no way to improve it.

The size of the city is almost beyond comprehension. There is some disagreement among scholars regarding its size, but most agree that twelve thousand furlongs equals fifteen hundred miles.

The text does not say whether the measurement was of one side of the city or of the circumference. If it was of one side of the city, as the text seems to suggest, the length, breath, and height of the city would each be fifteen hundred miles. If the measurement was of the circumference, the city would reach three hundred and seventy-five miles in every direction. In either case the city John saw was immense.

There has been much speculation about where such a large city can be located. Some scholars have speculated that the city will remain in orbit around the earth. The first half of verse 24 says, *And the nations of them which are saved shall walk in the light of it.* That can be taken to mean that the heavenly city will be in orbit. However, the last half of the verse says. . . . *and the kings of the earth do bring their glory and honour into it.* It would be most difficult for the kings of the earth bring their glory and honor into it if the city were in orbit.

There are other passages that indicate that the city will be located on earth. The prophet Isaiah wrote:

. . . the Lord of hosts shall reign in mount Zion, and in Jerusalem, and before his ancients gloriously (Isa. 24:23).

That means that the Lord of hosts will reign in Mount Zion in Jerusalem. That is certainly on the earth.

Revelation 5:10 says, *And hast made us unto our God kings and priests: and we shall reign on the earth.*

This verse tells us that God will reign on the earth and that we will reign with Him. That will be during the millennium. It is not likely that our reign with Christ will be moved to a city in orbit during eternity.

Another indication that the city will be located on the new earth is in verse 23. It says that God and Jesus will be resident in the city. . . . *for the glory of God did lighten it, and the Lamb is the light thereof.*

All of this indicates that the city will indeed be located on the earth.

The Measure of the Wall

17 And he measured the <u>wall thereof, an hundred and forty and four cubits, according to the measure of a man</u>, that is, of the angel.

The height of the wall around the city is quite low in comparison to the height of the city. Most scholars agree that the wall will be no more than two hundred and fifty feet high, but that is high enough. A higher wall will not be needed. It would only hide the beauty of the city. The wall will be garnished with all manner of precious stones, and on it will be displayed the names of the twelve apostles of the Lamb.

The City of Gold

18 And the building of the wall of it was of jasper: and <u>the city was pure gold, like unto clear glass.</u>

John must have been impressed with the golden glow of the city. In verse 18 he wrote that the city was pure gold, and in verse 21 he wrote that the street of the city was pure gold. The gold of the new Jerusalem will be unlike any gold that is found on earth. In both of the verses sighted John tells us that the gold is like clear glass.

The Beauty of the Wall

19 And the foundations of the wall of the city were <u>garnished with all manner of precious stones.</u> The first foundation was jasper; the second, sapphire; the third, a chalcedony; the fourth, an emerald;

20 The fifth, sardonyx; the sixth, sardius; the seventh, chrysolyte; the eighth, beryl; the ninth, a topaz; the tenth, a chrysoprasus; the eleventh, a jacinth; the twelfth, an amethyst.

Verses 19 and 20 tell us that the foundations of the city are garnished with twelve different precious stones. For information about the colors of these precious stones I quote from my book, *Spiritual Realities.*

The first foundation was jasper (diamond); the second, sapphire (blue, precious); the third, a chalcedony (pearly luster); the fourth, an emerald (translucent green); the fifth, sardonyx (red with white superimposed); the sixth, sardius (blood-red); the seventh, chrysolyte (yellow to greenish-yellow); the eighth, beryl (blue-green); the ninth, a topaz (yellow); the tenth, a chrysoprasus (apple-green); the eleventh, a jacinth (red); the twelfth, an amethyst (purple) (Rev. 21:18-20).

Not all authorities agree on the colors of the stones that will garnish the foundations of the wall of the city, but the above colors are accepted by most.

The Gates of Pearl

21 And the twelve gates were twelve pearls; every several gate was of one pearl: and the street of the city was pure gold, as it were transparent glass.

The pearl is the only jewel that is formed by suffering. When an oyster is injured, or when it gets a grain of sand inside its shell, it oozes a fluid that hardens and becomes a pearl. Each time we see the gates of pearl we will be reminded of the suffering of our Saviour on the cross.

God is the Temple

22 And I saw no temple therein:

for the Lord God Almighty and the Lamb
are the temple of it.

The glory of God was above the mercy seat in the tabernacle in the wilderness. After the temple was built in Jerusalem God was present in it, and people went there to worship. Every saved person is now a temple of God, for the Spirit of God dwells in them (1 Cor. 6:19).

There will be no temple in the new Jerusalem, for God and Jesus will be the temple. There will be no need of a temple, for there we will see God and worship Him face to face.

The Light of the City

23 And the city had no need of the
sun, neither of the moon, to shine in it:
for the glory of God did lighten it, and
the Lamb is the light thereof.

God was the source of light before the sun was created. In Genesis 1:3 God said, *Let there be light, and there was light.* That was before there was a sun. God did not create the sun and moon and stars until the fourth day of creation. Just as God was the light in the beginning, God will be the light in eternity. See Genesis 1:14-19.

The Saved Nations

24 And the nations of them which
are saved shall walk in the light of it:

and the kings of the earth do bring their glory and honour into it.

25 And <u>the gates of it shall not be shut at all by day: for there shall be no night there.</u>

26 <u>And they shall bring the glory and honour of the nations into it.</u>

27 And there shall in no wise enter into it any thing that defileth, neither whatsoever worketh abomination, or maketh a lie: but <u>they which are written in the Lamb's book of life.</u>

Verse 24 says that the nations that are saved will walk in the light of the city. Enough people will live through the tribulation to continue as nations on earth, but not all of them will be allowed to enter the millennial kingdom. In Matthew 25:31-35 we are told that when Christ comes in His glory He will judge the nations and will divide them (the nations) as a shepherd divides the sheep from the goats. The sheep nations will enter into the kingdom, and the goat nations will enter into everlasting punishment (verse 46).

The nations that are saved will walk in the light of the heavenly city and bring their glory and honor into it. All the people in the sheep nations will be converted, for Revelation 21:27 tells us that only those whose names are written in the Lamb's book of life will be allowed to enter the city.

Verses 24 through 27 deal with the nations that will be on earth in eternity. We must consider some facts that are often overlooked to understand these verses.

Fact #1. The earth will exist forever.

Who laid the foundations of the earth, that it should not be removed forever (Psa. 104:5).

Fact #2. Christ will reign on the earth forever.

And there was given him dominion, and glory, and a kingdom, that all people, nations, and languages, should serve him: his dominion is an everlasting dominion, which shall not pass away, and his kingdom that which shall not be destroyed (Daniel 7:14).

And he shall reign over the house of Jacob forever; and of his kingdom there shall be no end (Luke 1:33).

Christ will reign over Israel and all the other nations on this earth for a thousand years. Then He will turn the kingdom over to the Father, and they will reign jointly forever.

Then cometh the end, when he shall have delivered up the kingdom to God, even the Father; when he shall have put down all rule and all authority and power.

For he must reign, till he hath put all enemies under his feet (1 Cor. 15:24-25).

Fact #3. There will be nations on earth forever, and they will serve God throughout all eternity.

And many nations shall come, and say, Come, and let us go up to the mountain of the LORD, and to the house of the God of Jacob; and he will teach us of his ways, and we will walk in his paths: for the law shall go forth of Zion, and the word of the LORD from Jerusalem (Mic. 4:2).

Chapter 22

Introduction to Chapter 22

*C*hapter 22 is a continuation of a vision John saw in chapter 21. In chapter 21 the angel showed John the outside of the new Jerusalem. In this chapter he showed him the inside of the city. The first vision John saw in this chapter was of the river of life. The chapter ends with a promise and a prayer.

Contents of Chapter 22

1. The crystal river (verse 1)
2. The tree of life (verse 2)
3. The occupation of God's people (verse 3)
4. God will be visible (verse 4)
5. The eternal reign (verse 5)
6. The epilogue (verse 6)
7. The repeated promise (verse 7)
8. John's testimony (verses 8, 9)
9. Too late to change (verses 10-12)
10. The alpha and omega (verse 13)
11. The right to the tree of life (verse 14)
12. The condition of the wicked (verse 15)
13. The dual nature of Jesus (verse 16)

14. The final invitation (verse 17)
15. The sacred Book (verses 18, 19)
16. A promise and a prayer (verse 20)
17. John's salutation (verse 21)

The Crystal River

1 And he shewed me a pure <u>river of water of life, clear as crystal, proceeding out of the throne of God and of the Lamb.</u>

The river John saw flowing from the throne of God and the Lamb is more beautiful than any river on earth. It is crystal clear and pure. It will never be polluted, and it will never stop flowing.

The river is real, but it is also symbolic. It is called the water of life. Without water on earth life would not be possible. Without spiritual water spiritual life is not possible. As the river John saw flows from the throne of God, the water of life flows from the Son of God.

It is difficult to grasp the beauty of the river that flows between golden avenues with trees of life growing along its shores. Our attention is focused on this one river, but there will be many other rivers and streams in Heaven. The Psalmist wrote of rivers and streams that will make glad the city of God.

There is a river, the streams whereof shall make glad the city of God, the holy place of the tabernacles of the most High (Psa. 46:4).

The Tree of Life

2 In the midst of the street of it, and
on either side of the river, was there the
tree of life, which bare twelve manner
of fruits, and yielded her fruit every
month: and the leaves of the tree were
for the healing of the nations.

The first mention of the tree of life is in Genesis 2:9. That tree grew in the midst of the garden of Eden. After Adam and Eve sinned and were driven from the garden, cherubim with flaming swords guarded the tree of life so they could not eat of it and live forever in their fallen state (Gen. 3:24).

In eternity God's people will have access to the tree of life. The leaves of the tree of life are symbolic of the health people will enjoy in eternity. There will be no curse on the new earth, and people will never become ill. The twelve manners of fruit the tree will bear will be for people to eat and enjoy every month in the year.

The Occupation of God's People

3 And there shall be no more curse:
but the throne of God and of the Lamb
shall be in it; and his servants shall serve
him:

People in Heaven will not be idle. There will

be much to do in the service of God. They will never grow tired, and they will never have to go to bed, for there will be no night there.

The church will reign with Christ and be involved in the government of the earth. The Jews and saved Gentile nations will live on the new earth. They will build houses, cultivate the land, build cities, construct roads and bridges, and conduct themselves much as people now do on the present earth.

The curse will be lifted, and the world will be the paradise that God intended it to be in the beginning. There will be no devil to tempt, and there will be no sin. There will be no sorrow, and no death. People will enjoy serving God and taking care of the perfect new earth as Adam was commanded to do when God placed him in the garden of Eden in the beginning (Gen. 2:15).

God Will be Visible

4 And <u>they shall see his face;</u> and <u>his name shall be in their foreheads.</u>

God is now invisible to us. No man can see His face and live, but He will be visible in eternity. At last the redeemed will see God face to face. His name will be upon their foreheads. They will serve Him, and He will claim them as His own dear children.

The Eternal Reign

5 And <u>there shall be no night there</u>;

and they need no candle, neither light of the sun; for the <u>Lord God giveth them light: and they shall reign for ever and ever.</u>

Verse 5 begins by saying, *there shall be no night there.* God will be the source of light in Heaven. The Bible says that God is light and there is no darkness in Him at all (1 John 1:5). Darkness cannot remain in God's presence.

The verse ends by saying, *they shall reign for ever and ever.* The new Heaven and the new earth will abide forever, and we are reminded that the redeemed will reign with God the Father and God the Son forever.

The Epilogue

6 And he said unto me, <u>These sayings are faithful and true:</u> and <u>the Lord God of the holy prophets sent his angel to shew unto his servants the things which must shortly be done.</u>

Verse 6 says, *These sayings are faithful and true.* Just as the other books of the Bible are true, The Revelation is true. This verse is an affirmation of the first verse in Chapter 1. There we are told that God gave The Revelation to John to show to His servants things that were soon to come to pass. In the above verse we read, *God of the holy prophets sent his angel <u>to shew unto his</u>*

servants the things which must shortly be done.

The Repeated Promise

7 Behold, I come quickly: blessed is he that keepeth the sayings of the prophecy of this book.

Four times in The Revelation Jesus affirms that He will come quickly (Rev. 3:11; 22:7; 22:12 and 22:20). How can we reconcile His promise to come quickly with the fact that more than two thousand years have passed since the promise was made? We must remember that a thousand years is no more than a day to our heavenly Father. The time seems long to us, but it is not long to Him.

The Second Coming of Christ is certainly nearer now than it was when Jesus promised to come quickly. The many prophecies that have been fulfilled in our day indicate that His coming is drawing near. He may come at any hour of any day.

John's Testimony

8 And I John saw these things, and heard them. And when I had heard and seen, I fell down to worship before the feet of the angel which shewed me these things.

9 Then saith he unto me, See thou

do it not: for I am thy fellowservant, and of thy brethren the prophets, and of them which keep the sayings of this book: worship God.

John affirmed that he had written about what he had seen and heard as he had been told to do in chapter 1, verse 2. Then he confessed that he had fallen down to worship the angel that had showed him the visions.

Perhaps John was so overcome by what he had seen and heard that he forgot he was not supposed to worship angels. The angel rebuked him and reminded him that he was not to be worshiped, for he was also a servant of God.

Too Late to Change

10 And he saith unto me, <u>Seal not the sayings of the prophecy of this book:</u> for the time is at hand.

11 <u>He that is unjust, let him be unjust still: and he which is filthy, let him be filthy still: and he that is righteous, let him be righteous still: and he that is holy, let him be holy still.</u>

12. And, behold, I come quickly; and <u>my reward is with me, to give every man according as his work shall be.</u>

The angel told John not to seal the prophecy, he had given him because the time would come when it would be too late for people to change. Whatever their condition at the coming of the Lord, it would remain the same. Verse 11 says, *He that is unjust, let him be unjust still: and he which is filthy, let him be filthy still: and he that is righteous, let him be righteous still: and he that is holy, let him be holy still.*

Verse 12 reminds us that the Lord will come quickly and judge everyone according to their works.

The Alpha and Omega

13 I am Alpha and Omega, the beginning and the end, the first and the last.

We are reminded four times in The Revelation that Jesus is the Alpha and Omega. This phrase is given at the beginning of the book and at the close of the book. It is found in chapter 1 two times, in chapter 21 one time, and in chapter 22 one time.

The Right to the Tree of Life

14 Blessed are they that do his commandments, that they may have right to the tree of life, and may enter in through the gates into the city.

The nations on earth will have to earn the blessings of God. There is an illuminating passage in Zechariah that tells us that in the new earth there will be penalties for not serving the Lord.

> *And it shall come to pass, that every one that is left of all the nations which came against Jerusalem shall even go up from year to year to worship the King, the LORD of hosts, and to keep the feast of tabernacles.*
>
> *And it shall be, that whoso will not come up of all the families of the earth unto Jerusalem to worship the King, the LORD of hosts, even upon them shall be no rain (Zech. 14:16, 17).*
>
> *In that day shall there be upon the bells of the horses, HOLINESS UNTO THE LORD; and the pots in the LORD'S house shall be like the bowls before the altar.*
>
> *Yea, every pot in Jerusalem and in Judah shall be holiness unto the LORD of hosts: . . . (Zech. 14:20, 21).*

The Condition of the Wicked

> *15 For without are dogs, and sorcerers, and whoremongers, and murderers, and idolaters, and whosoever loveth and maketh a lie.*

Idolaters were called dogs in the Old Testament. People who are guilty of this and other sins are clearly identified in this verse. All the wicked described in verse 15 are outside the circle of God's family. They have never repented of their sins and asked Jesus to save them, and they will remain in outer darkness throughout eternity.

The Dual Nature of Jesus

16 I Jesus have sent mine angel to testify unto you these things in the churches. I am the root and <u>the offspring of David, and the bright and morning star.</u>

Verse 16 tells us that Jesus was the offspring of David. The virgin mother of Jesus was of the house of David. That made Him the offspring of David. Being born of a woman made Him the son of man. Being begotten of the Holy Spirit made Him the Son of God.

As the offspring of David, He is heir to David's throne. As the son of man He bore our sins and our sorrows. As the Son of God He is the bright and morning star, and He will reign with His Father forever.

The Final Invitation

17 <u>And the Spirit and the bride say, Come. And let him that heareth say, Come. And let him that is athirst come.</u>

And whosoever will, let him take the
water of life freely.

In verse 17 it is almost as if Jesus said, "John, The Revelation is almost finished, but before you close the book, I want to again invite men to come to me and be saved one more time. I do not want anyone to believe that they are left out, so I want you to tell them that the Holy Spirit is inviting them to come to me and be saved. Tell them that the church is inviting them to come to me and be saved. Tell them that saved people are inviting them to come to me and be saved, and tell them that every time they hear the Word of God they are invited to come to me and be saved. John, add this also, everyone who is thirsty is invited to come and drink of the water of life freely."

The Sacred Book

18 For I testify unto every man that heareth the words of the prophecy of this book, If any man shall add unto these things, God shall add unto him the plagues that are written in this book:

19 And if any man shall take away from the words of the book of this prophecy, God shall take away his part out of the book of life, and out of the holy city, and from the things which are written in this book.

John knows that what he has written is the inspired Word of God. In the first chapter of The Revelation he wrote that the Alpha and Omega had commissioned him to write the Book. Here he says that any one who tampers with what he has written will be judged and punished.

A Promise and a Prayer

20 He which testifieth these things saith, <u>Surely I come quickly.</u> Amen. <u>Even so, come, Lord Jesus.</u>

In verse 20 Jesus says again that He will come quickly. John wrote *Amen* and closed the verse with the prayer, *Even so, come, Lord Jesus.* Only John's salutation is now needed to close the book.

John's Salutation

21 The grace of our Lord Jesus Christ be with you all. Amen.

Appendix

*T*he purpose of the appendix is to emphasize the joyful aspects of The Revelation and to show that all its visions and predictions are not somber. Triumph and victory are woven like threads of gold through the dark tapestry of the Book. It is a Book of lights and shadows. It is about the judgments that will come upon the earth in the last days and it is about the future glory the people of God will enjoy.

Across the bosom of every storm there is a rainbow of promise. The voice of thunders and the rumble of earthquakes cannot hush the songs of praise and shouts of victory.

The letters to the seven churches show the trials the church will go through on earth, but when John was translated he saw the future glory of the church. He saw the church seated near the throne of God, clothed in robes of righteousness and wearing crowns of gold.

And he heard the four beast (seraphim) saying:

> . . . *Holy, holy, holy, Lord God Al-*
> *mighty, which was, and is, and is to come*
> (verse 8).

Then he was told that the seraphim give glory and honor and praise to God.

> *And when those beasts give glory*
> *and honour and thanks to him that sat*
> *on the throne, who liveth for ever and*
> *ever (verse 9).*

The seraphim have been giving praise to God through the centuries. Seven hundred and fifty-eight years before the birth of Christ Isaiah saw the seraphim before the throne of God and heard them saying almost the same words that John heard.

> . . . *Holy, holy, holy, is the LORD of*
> *hosts: the whole earth is full of his glory*
> *(Isa. 6:3).*

Following the praise of the seraphim the church, represented by the four and twenty elders, praise God and cast their crowns before His throne.

> *10 The four and twenty elders fall*
> *down before him that sat on the throne,*
> *and worship him that liveth for ever and*
> *ever, and cast their crowns before the*

throne, saying,

11 Thou art worthy, O Lord, to receive glory and honour and power: for thou hast created all things, and for thy pleasure they are and were created (Rev. 4:10, 11).

There will be great sorrow and trouble on earth following the rapture of the church, but there will only be glory in Heaven.

In Revelation 5, after the Lamb is found worthy to open the scroll containing the title to the earth, there will be more rejoicing and praise.

8 And when he had taken the book, the four beasts and four and twenty elders fell down before the Lamb, having every one of them harps, and golden vials full of odours, which are the prayers of saints.

9 And they sung a new song, saying, Thou art worthy to take the book, and to open the seals thereof: for thou wast slain, and hast redeemed us to God by thy blood out of every kindred, and tongue, and people, and nation;

10 And hast made us unto our God kings and priests: and we shall reign on the earth.

11 And I beheld, and I heard the voice

of many angels round about the throne and the beasts and the elders: and the number of them was ten thousand times ten thousand, and thousands of thousands;

12 Saying with a loud voice, Worthy is the Lamb that was slain to receive power, and riches, and wisdom, and strength, and honour, and glory, and blessing.

13 And every creature which is in heaven, and on the earth, and under the earth, and such as are in the sea, and all that are in them, heard I saying, Blessing, and honour, and glory, and power, be unto him that sitteth upon the throne, and unto the Lamb for ever and ever.

14 And the four beasts said, Amen. And the four and twenty elders fell down and worshipped him that liveth for ever and ever.

Chapter 7 tells of rejoicing after the sealing of the 144 thousand of the twelve tribes of Israel. John saw a great multitude rejoicing in Heaven. There we are told that John saw a multitude that had been saved from all the tribes of the earth. Apparently they will be saved by the testimony of the sealed men of Israel.

9 After this I beheld, and, lo, a great

multitude, which no man could number, of all nations, and kindreds, and people, and tongues, stood before the throne, and before the Lamb, clothed with white robes, and palms in their hands;

10 And cried with a loud voice, saying, Salvation to our God which sitteth upon the throne, and unto the Lamb.

11 And all the angels stood round about the throne, and about the elders and the four beasts, and fell before the throne on their faces, and worshipped God,

12 Saying, Amen: Blessing, and glory, and wisdom, and thanksgiving, and honour, and power, and might, be unto our God for ever and ever. Amen.

Chapter 14 gives a view of the 144 thousand sealed men of Israel with the Lamb of God on the heavenly Mount Zion singing the praises of God.

1 AND I looked, and lo, a Lamb stood on the mount Sion, and with an hundred forty and four thousand, having his Father's name written in their foreheads.

2 And I heard a voice from heaven as the voice of many waters, and as the voice of a great thunder: and I heard the voice of harpers harping with their harps:

3 And they sung as it were a new song before the throne, and before the four beasts, and the elders: and no man could learn that song but the hundred and forty and four thousand, which were redeemed from the earth.

Revelation 19 gives the four hallelujahs, and in chapter 21, we have the beginning of eternity. In that chapter John saw a new Heaven and a new earth. He saw the new Jerusalem coming down from God out of Heaven, and he heard a great voice from Heaven, saying,

. . . Behold, the tabernacle of God is with men, and he will dwell with them, and they shall be his people, and God himself shall be with them, and be their God (verse 3).

Verse 4 tells us that there will be no more death or sorrow, pain, or crying, and God will wipe away all tears. That means that in Heaven we will have eternal health and happiness.

Revelation 22 tells of the comforts, the provision, and the health we will enjoy in Heaven. The curse that has been on this earth since the fall of Adam and Eve will be removed (verses 1-5). The glory, rejoicing, praise, and victory in The Revelation are covered in these verses as well.

1 AND he shewed me a pure river of

water of life, *clear as crystal, proceed-ing out of the throne of God and of the Lamb.*

2 In the midst of the street of it, and on either side of the river, was there the tree of life, which bare twelve manner of fruits, and yielded her fruit every month: and the leaves of the tree were for the healing of the nations.

3 And there shall be no more curse: but the throne of God and of the Lamb shall be in it; and his servants shall serve him:

4 And they shall see his face; and his name shall be in their foreheads.

5 And there shall be no night there; and they need no candle, neither light of the sun; for the Lord God giveth them light: and they shall reign for ever and ever.

Books by Dr. Louis Arnold

Thousands praise Dr. Arnold's books, and hundreds order them before they are off the press. People love his novels and his Bible study books.

Great Inspirational Fiction

Readers appreciate the strong characters Dr. Arnold creates, his powers of description, and his gripping, emotion-filled stories.

Legend of Old Faithful, hardcover $19.99

Out of the Night, hardcover $19.99

Fathoms Deep, hardcover $19.99

Riverman, softcover . . . .$ 9.99

Riverman (Audio) read by author $12.99

Sunshine Valley, softcover . . . .$ 9.99

Euroclydon, softcover . . . .$ 9.99

Lucinda of Perryville, softcover . . . .$ 9.99

A Girl Named Candy, softcover . . . .$ 9.99

The Angel of Dragonpoint, softcover. . . . .$ 9.99

Birdman, softcover . . . .$ 9.99

Other Arnold Books

Israeli Countdown to Eternity, softcover . . . .$ 9.99

When Will the Tribulation Begin? softcover $9.99

Spiritual Realities, softcover . . . .$ 9.99

Day Starters (best selling devotional) softcover . . . . .$ 9.99

Family and Friends Cookbook (J. Arnold) . . . .$ 9.99

Great Preachers I Have Known, softcover. . . . . . .$ 9.99

Arnold Publications --2440 Bethel Road --Nicholasville, KY 40356 Phone 1-800-854-8571